EASTER

EASTER

Its Story and Meaning

ALAN WATTS

With Illustrations by the Author

Afterword by Joan Watts

New World Library
Novato, California

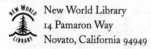 New World Library
14 Pamaron Way
Novato, California 94949

Text design by Tona Pearce Myers

Library of Congress Cataloging-in-Publication data is available.

First New World Library printing, March 2023
ISBN 978-1-60868-858-6
Ebook ISBN 978-1-60868-859-3
Printed in Canada on 100% postconsumer-waste recycled paper

 New World Library is proud to be a Gold Certified Environmentally
Responsible Publisher. Publisher certification awarded by Green Press
Initiative.

10 9 8 7 6 5 4 3 2 1

To Joan

with very much love from

    her Father –

    Alan W. Watts

March 7th, 1950.

You may not be able to understand all of this book just yet. But I have written it for you because I do not want you ever to be afraid of death, whether it be the death of people or the death of old times which we have loved. I want you to understand that all kinds of death are the source of new life, and that if we do not die, we cannot live. See how God uses dead leaves to make good soil for the flowers.

THE RESURRECTION

Albrecht Dürer, 1510

CONTENTS

ILLUSTRATIONS

EASTER

ST. THOMAS TOUCHING THE WOUNDS OF THE RISEN CHRIST
THE WOMEN AND THE ANGELS AT THE EMPTY TOMB
(from *Salzburg Pericopes* [Salzburg, around 1020], Bayerische
Staatsbibliothek Munich, Clm 15713, fol. 29v)
Page 78

"DO NOT CLING TO ME!"
The Risen Christ appears to St. Mary Magdalene
(Martin Schongauer, © Bridgeman Images)
Page 90

EARLY-MORNING EASTER MASS
(Alan Watts, © Joan Watts)
Page 120

EXPLANATIONS OF THE HEADPIECES

drawn by the author

Chapter 1

WHAT IS EASTER?: Wheat with butterfly and caterpillar. Explanation in the first two paragraphs of the chapter.

Chapter 2

THE MYSTERIOUS EGG: The World-Egg lying upon the waters of chaos, with the bird symbol of the divinity flying above.

Chapter 3

SPRING AND THE SUN CYCLE: The Winged Disk, Egyptian symbol of Ra, the Sun God.

Chapter 4

THE GODS WHO DIED AND ROSE: These were the "vegeta-tion" gods of the corn and vine, whose symbolism is summed up in Christ — the True Vine and the Bread of Life. The symbol is formed upon the ancient monogram of the Name of Christ — the Greek letters XP (*chi rho*), being the first two letters of Christos.

Chapter 5

THE ANCIENT MYSTERIES: The Tree of Life — Christian version of the tree symbolism and the life-through-death theme so prevalent in the ancient mysteries. From the Body of Christ his life-giving Blood falls upon the wheat (representing man), and from the foot of the tree flows the stream of the water of life.

Chapter 6

THE LAMB OF GOD: Explained within the chapter.

Chapter 7

THE EASTER CALENDAR: The symbol shows the sundial surrounded by the signs of the Zodiac — representing Time. The shadow on the sundial points to the hour of dawn, and against it is Aries, the sign of the Ram, the constellation where the sun was anciently found at the vernal equinox. The Dove of the Holy Spirit descends upon the sundial, because the sanctification of Time is the basic idea of the Christian Year.

Chapter 8

"HE IS RISEN!": Christ as a radiant cross rising from the empty tomb. The Greek letters round the cross, IC (*iota sigma*) XC (*chi sigma*) NIKA (*nu iota kappa alpha*), mean "Jesus Christ Victor," and denote Christ triumphant over death.

Chapter 9

A THOUSAND YEARS AFTER: The Paschal Candle in the waters of the font. Explained in the chapter.

Chapter 10

EASTER IN FOLKLORE: About the cross, reading counterclockwise, are (a) the bowl and pitcher for the Maundy custom of foot-washing: (b) the Good Friday hot cross bun; (c) the fire and water of the Holy Saturday customs; and (d) the Easter egg.

Chapter 11

THE SECRET OF THE SYMBOLS: The fish, symbol of Christ, descending and ascending from the "material waters" in representation of the two divine acts of creation and salvation.

PREFACE

The story of Easter is not simply a Christian story. It is true that for more than fifteen hundred years the feast of Easter has celebrated the resurrection of Jesus Christ. But not only is the very name "Easter" the name of an ancient and non-Christian deity; the season itself has also, from time immemorial, been the occasion of rites and observances having to do with the mystery of death and resurrection among peoples differing widely in race and religion. As a result, the full story of Easter is a most complex mixture of history and mythology — so much so that the difficult task of distinguishing between the two is far beyond the scope of a short book.

For orthodox Christianity the resurrection of Christ is, without question, a historical fact, and pre-Christian "Easters" are at best mythical foreshadowings of this most wonderful event in all time. Yet many who call themselves Christians concur with the intellectual temper of the modern age in regarding the resurrection of their Master as sublime mythology, and no more. A very strong case can be made for the truth of the orthodox

Christian belief, but the proper statement of the arguments in its favor would take up so large a part of the book as to carry it far beyond the purpose of the series of works to which it belongs. This purpose is to tell the stories of the great religious festivals, not to arrive at historical judgments about them.

However, the orthodox Christian need feel no offense if the story of Christ is somewhat uncritically included with tales which are obviously myths. For if the resurrection of Christ is a fact of history it is *also* a myth. A myth is not a lie; it is not a falsification of history. Myth is a special kind of language, quite distinct from historical or scientific language. The purpose of myth is not to relate concrete facts and events which take place in time and space; it is rather to symbolize certain realities beyond time and space, realities of the divine and eternal order. In this sense of the word, no orthodox Christian will deny that the story of Christ is mythological as well as historical, for he believes that the very events of the life of Jesus differ from other events for the precise reason that, among other things, they reveal the mind of God.

Looked at from this point of view, the study of myth is one of the most exciting and worthwhile tasks in the world. It is exciting because, on the surface, it is a realm of fabulous wonders, of story and poetry, comprising much of the most splendid and absorbing literature which the past has handed down to us. It is worthwhile because, unlike modern fiction (great as much of it may be), myths are not the deliberate inventions of individuals. They arise in the mind of man as spontaneously and as naturally as his dreams, to represent, as psychoanalysis has shown us, things that are going on in the very depths of his psychic life — depths where, as the Christian would say, the soul has contact with the Holy Spirit of God.

So far as I am aware, a book of this kind has never been attempted before, surprising as this may be in view of the important place which Easter holds in the Christian Year. There is an abundance of works on the resurrection of Christ, on the mythologies of the death-and-resurrection gods, and on folkways where those peculiar to Easter are noted. But there is no general description of the history and the celebration of Easter even in its Christian context alone, much less one which takes into account its pre-Christian "types."

The material for this book has been gathered from a great number of sources, all of which have been so rich that it has been a problem to decide how much of it to select for a brief work of this kind. Thus the reader will almost invariably think of phases of the Easter theme which have not been mentioned, having had to be excluded for lack of space. The complexity of the material, the novelty of the attempt, and the problem of explaining ancient forms of imagery to a world whose mentality has now so little in common with these bygone times, will account for many imperfections in the book of which the author is acutely aware.

In particular, I am conscious of not having done justice to that interpretation of Easter which is traditionally Christian. But drafts of the manuscript which attempted to do so became heavily overloaded with "homiletic" and "theological" material, seriously squeezing out the simple telling of the story. Couched in its traditional language, this interpretation may be stated briefly enough — as is often done from the pulpit on an Easter morning — but to the average modern man this language is almost wholly unintelligible.

I am indebted to the Oxford University Press for their kind permission to quote translations by Canon Winfred Douglas of certain verses from Latin hymns.

My special thanks are due to the publisher for the most painstaking and minute criticism of the manuscript during its preparation.

Alan W. Watts
Evanston, Illinois
October 1949

I

WHAT IS EASTER?

B efore it can come to life as a plant, the seed must be buried in the earth. Before it can soar into the air upon brilliant wings, the caterpillar must enter the long sleep of its chrysalis tomb. Before the splendor of spring, all the earth is shrouded in the gray, cold death of winter. "Unless a grain of corn fall into the ground and die, it remains alone. But if it dies, it brings forth much fruit." In those words Christ summed up the strange truth that life is ever dependent upon death.

Buried in its earthy grave, the single seed becomes the full head of corn or wheat. A multitude of grains are gathered together and "die" under the grinding stone, and out of this second death comes bread, the "staff of life." Yet again, the loaf of bread is "buried" in the human body. Its life passes on into the growing man, and the waste returns to the earth to fertilize the soil and give life once more to the buried seed.

That, in brief, is the theme of the Easter story, of the rising from death of him who called himself the Bread of Life. For this reason, the whole point of Easter is lost if the feast is taken out of its context. The resurrection of Christ into eternal life is an event stripped of its meaning if it be set apart from the sacrificial death which preceded it. As a river lives and flows only because it pours itself out into the ocean, so the condition of Easter is the Good Friday Crucifixion, and so the condition of eternal life is that incessant "dying to oneself" which is called love.

The story of Easter cannot, therefore, be told apart from the story of the Passion. The two events are inseparable in the life of Christ, and wherever and whenever men have kept the springtime feast of life's everlasting renewal, they have never failed to represent its dependence upon death. Easter is, indeed, far older than Christianity. However much Christianity may have enriched the feast in both meaning and reality, the same essential theme has been celebrated under many different names and circumstances. But the distinguishing and all-important mark of this Easter theme is not resurrection alone, but death *and* resurrection — the coming of life out of sacrifice.

What, then, *is* Easter? In the first place, it is the feast at which Christians commemorate the resurrection of Christ the third day after his death by crucifixion. It is the greatest feast of the Christian Year, celebrated with the utmost joy, because it promises a like resurrection to all who have accepted the Faith of Christ.

In the second place, Easter — by whatever name it may be known — is a theme common to almost every religion and every people. Usually, but not always, observed with special rites at a certain time of year, it is the theme that through death man can enter an eternal life. Sometimes the "death" in question is a physical death. But at other times it is, and has long been, understood as a "psychic death" — that is, as self-denial, self-sacrifice, or self-forgetting, while yet in the midst of life.

When we think of Easter as a universal theme, it is so widespread that its story cannot always be a history. We cannot always find connecting links between the various forms of the Easter theme, as if the original idea had been carried by travelers to different parts of the world. On the contrary, the Easter theme of death and resurrection seems to have grown up all by itself in the most distant times and places. But though it is not always a history, it is nearly always a story rather than a doctrine or an idea.

For the great majority of men do not think with abstract ideas. They think with colorful images or with concrete facts. They know the abstract, the spiritual, the world of ideas and principles only in so far as it is *clothed* in some vivid and moving form. Thus the Easter theme is expressed not so much in doctrines as in stories, myths, and dramatic rituals having to do with the adventures of hero-gods and other symbolic figures.

At first sight it is surprising to find so many of these stories and symbols of death and resurrection in so many different places. The points of resemblance between the Christ story, on the one hand, and the myth and ritual of ancient and "pagan" cults, on the other, is at times startling enough to look like a conspiracy. Indeed, a few of the early Fathers of the Church regarded these resemblances as cunning contrivances of the Devil, specially prearranged to confuse the faithful. But there are two much more reasonable explanations.

One, adopted by some of the other Fathers, was that since the Spirit of God is everywhere, he is always trying to enlighten the minds of men. Working from within their hearts, he influences their imaginations to produce Christlike stories symbolizing the truths of God. For the whole history of Christ is understood by the Church as a symbol of the relation of God to man. Thus, by the power of the Spirit, the same relation is foreshadowed in the myths of the ancient gods.

The other explanation, which might be true at the same time as the first, is that man's imagination everywhere employs the same mythical and religious images — with superficial variations — just as a house built in China is basically the same as a house built in America. Wherever he is found, man has two arms and two legs, a head, heart, and stomach. As his body is everywhere of the same basic pattern, so also is his mind and imagination. If the student of philosophy or religion finds similar *ideas* in all parts of the world, he should not be surprised to find similar *images* in use by those unaccustomed to abstract thought.

Obviously the death-and-resurrection theme, myth, or image, does not enter into man's imagination as a baseless and meaningless fantasy. There must be something underneath it, some desire, some inner truth, for which it provides the material clothing. It has been suggested that it is really a story about the sun or the crops. The setting and rising of the sun, the sowing and sprouting of the corn, are dramatized as the actions of hero-gods — Christ, Osiris, Ra, Tammuz, and Adonis, all of whom undergo death and resurrection.

In a way this is true, for even to the Christian it is certain that the sun rises and the corn grows by the power of God. But the myths are not simply stories about the sun or the crops. People — even primitive people — would hardly look at their corn and say, "Sh! This is dangerous stuff, and we must only talk about it in symbols. Hereafter no one must say that the corn comes up in spring. We must say that Osiris has returned from death!" There is something much more in the Easter theme than a mere complex sign for an obvious natural event.

It is also thought that the stories of death and resurrection are simply translations into fantasy of man's deep-rooted wish for personal immortality. Religion, however, must insist that the story of Easter represents far more than a mere hope. For if the resurrection is nothing more than wishful thinking, the interest of Easter must become purely sentimental. The telling of its story will be no more than a review of the quaint superstitions, the crude hopes, and the unscientific opinions of our ancient forefathers. In a sophisticated and scientific world, Easter will — if this be true — live on as a feast only for little children and for very simple, ignorant folk. It will be a convenient excuse for colored eggs, cute bunnies, and new hats — a dying flame fanned into life by the commercial needs of poultry farmers, toy manufacturers, and milliners.

But what does science know about the inner life of man? Why, it does not even have a way of looking at it, much less finding out anything about it! If the eyes cannot turn round and see themselves, how much less can the mysterious spirit which looks through the eyes see itself. There is no mirror, no microscope, no test tube, no X-ray camera, whereby a scientist can know the very act of knowing. He can observe everything in the world save his own inmost self.

Although the language of images suggests that the spiritual world is extended in space and time, it really lies within this unknown center of our being. "The kingdom of heaven is within you." The extension in space and time belongs to the images, not to the Spirit which they represent. The imagery of death and resurrection is saying, then, that the inmost source and center of man's life is an eternal Spirit. It remains invisible and unknown, because it "forgets" itself in loving and creating us, so that by a kind of "death" (and is not love death to self?) it gives us life.

There is a very obvious suggestion of some such idea as this, even if the Easter theme be held to be the story of the annual death and resurrection of the corn spirit. For does not the grain give us life by "sacrificing itself" under the millstone? If some of the ancient heroes of the Easter theme — Tammuz or Osiris — were indeed the corn spirit, it is perhaps significant that, like the grain, they died involuntarily. On the other hand, the supreme Easter Hero, Christ, died willingly — to reveal that the true giver of life is not the blind corn but the Living God.

In some remote future the last grain of corn will shrivel away forever, for the corn is a finite creature like ourselves. But if our life is not from the corn, but from the Living and Eternal God, we may be sure that we are living an eternal life. "But as touching the resurrection of the dead, have ye not read that which was spoken unto you by God, saying, 'I *am* the God of Abraham, and the God of Isaac, and the God of Jacob'? God is not God of the dead, but of the living: for all live unto him."

THE RESURRECTION *(detail)*

El Greco, 16th century
Madrid, Prado

2

THE MYSTERIOUS EGG

We must begin with the egg. The egg is not, indeed, the most important thing about Easter, but it is certainly the first memory of the Feast which most of us recollect from childhood. Furthermore, an egg is a beginning, and Easter is a feast of beginnings, of the emergence of life from darkness and death.

Few Christian historians seem to have any clear ideas about the origin of the Easter egg. Some say that it was traditional to bless and eat eggs at Easter because they were not allowed to be eaten during the fast time of Lent, which Easter brings to an end.

Others trace it to St. Augustine's comparison of the egg with the virtue of hope, and in particular with the hope of eternal life, because the egg, like hope, is that which has not yet come to fruition. But the colored eggs for which American children hunt around the house on Easter Morning, and the gaily wrapped chocolate eggs which are (or used to be) the special Easter treat for English children, have a much more ancient and mysterious history.

The problem of the Easter egg takes us back to some of the oldest known civilizations on earth — to ancient Egypt and India, where the symbol of an egg plays an important part in mythical accounts of the creation of the world. The mythology of Egypt is a most confusing subject, not only because there are so many gods, each having many different names, but also because there are so many different systems of gods, each with its own chief god. Sometimes the chief, or *erpat*, of the gods is named Geb, he whose body is the earth, whose feminine counterpart is Nut, the sky, and whose son is Osiris, the lord of the Tuat, or underworld. The great work of Geb and Nut was the production of a mighty egg — the germ from which the whole universe was born. Out of this egg came the fabulous Bennu bird, or phoenix, symbol of the sun, a bird which Christianity has adopted as a representation of Christ because of the peculiar way in which it is supposed to die and come to life again.

For the phoenix is said to die by setting fire to its own nest and burning itself to ashes. In these ashes is found an egg from which the phoenix hatches once again, a procedure which is said to repeat every fourteen hundred years! In ancient art the phoenix is shown in a form somewhat similar to the peacock. Now the peacock appears constantly in Christian churches — in stonework, embroidery, painting, and engraving — as a symbol of Christ's resurrection from his own voluntary death. The phoenix is connected with the sun because of the way in which it seems to die at sunset in a blaze of flame, to rise again into life at the following dawn. Likewise the Church hails Christ: "O Day-spring, Brightness of the Light everlasting, and Sun of righteousness: come and enlighten them that sit in darkness and the shadow of death."

Another Egyptian system calls the chief of the gods Ptah, and an ancient drawing shows him seated on his throne before a potter's wheel, upon which he is fashioning a golden egg. An Egyptian scripture refers to him as "Father of beginnings, and creator of the egg of the Sun and Moon."

Hindu mythology also tells us of the World-Egg, which was formed in the "waters of chaos" before the universe and time had begun. (Water is almost always used as the symbol for the original chaos because it is formless and fluid.) This was a great egg of gold from which came forth Prajapati, the father of gods, men, and all creatures. Another version of the myth states that Prajapati himself created the World-Egg out of his own sweat and that the upper half of its shell contains the heavens and the lower half the earth. A Hindu scripture says: "In the beginning this world was merely non-being. It was existent. It developed. It turned into an egg. It lay for a period of a year. It was split asunder. One of the two eggshell parts became silver, one gold. That which was of silver is the earth. That which was of gold is the sky. What was the outer membrane is the mountains. What was the inner membrane is cloud and mist. What were the veins are the rivers. What was the fluid within is the ocean. Now, what was born therefrom is yonder sun."

In the Phoenician story of the creation an egg was likewise formed in Mōt, the primeval waters, and, splitting open, the two parts of the shell became heaven and earth.

Perhaps there is no *historical* connection between the modern Easter egg and the World-Egg of ancient mythology. Indeed, there are no records of the use of Easter eggs in Western Europe before the fifteenth century, although the custom of coloring eggs at Easter has been found in an African tribe once Christian but long since converted to Mohammedanism. Possibly the custom found its way into Europe through warriors returning from the Crusades. We do not know. But in the world of symbolism and mythology, historical connections are of little importance. The point is that, apart from surface differences, the human mind is of the same essential nature in all times and places. As a result, it represents its unconscious depths, its hidden workings, with symbols which are ever the same. For the most part symbols come into being not through historical tradition but through *association*. That is to say, the human mind more or less unconsciously and automatically connects (or associates) its inner workings and states with certain outward objects. Moreover, what could be more natural and obvious than the connection between an egg and ideas or feelings of birth, new life, and creation? It is by no mere flight of private fancy that we associate our Easter egg with this mysterious World-Egg, this original germ from which all life proceeds, and whose shell is the firmament — the ancient word for the limits of space, which our own scientists believe to be curved!

But why should Easter, the Feast of Resurrection, be connected with a symbol having to do with the creation of the universe? Because there is an obvious parallel between the rising of Christ from death, and the rising of the universe from the original darkness of chaos and nonbeing. We shall see, too, that there is also a connection between the voluntary sacrificial death of Christ and the divine creative act which brought the world into being. For the moment, we may note that the egg is a symbol of death and life alike. It is a symbol of death in so far as it is a shell or tomb in which the life-germ is imprisoned. It is a symbol of life in so far as it is the source of a new creature.

The mythologies which describe the first god as fashioning the World-Egg carry the suggestion that, in making the egg, the god enters into it and then emerges from it in a new form. The egg of Geb and Nut produces the divine Sun-Bird, and, coming to birth, the Sun replaces both earth and sky as the Supreme Lord. Hindu mythology tells of Prajapati both forming and emerging from the egg. Likewise the phoenix, dying in the fire, leaves an egg from which he himself is once more hatched. We shall see that this element of the myth is of the highest importance.

Although we have decided to begin from the egg, we cannot avoid the immemorial riddle, "Which came the first, egg or hen?" According to no less an authority than St. Thomas Aquinas, one of the greatest of all Christian theologians, the argument is heavily in favor of the hen. "Every imperfect thing," he wrote, "must needs be preceded by some perfect thing: for seed is from some animal or plant."

The various myths are inclined to agree with St. Thomas. Egyptian mythology represents Geb as Kenkenur, "the Great Cackler" or Gander — a bird which is seen resting on the head of this god in Egyptian art. So also, in some versions of the Hindu myth, the World-Egg it said to be laid by Hamsa, the Divine Gander or Swan, which is a symbol for Brahma — the Supreme Divinity. Thus a common theme of Hindu art is the gander or swan floating on the waters of chaos with the World-Egg beneath him. In the Finnish epic known as the *Kalevala*, the earth, sky, sun, moon, and clouds are said to have been formed from the broken eggs of a teal sent by Ukko, the highest god, to nest upon the knee of the Water-Mother.

Much nearer to our own time we find the World-Egg appearing again in the fantastic symbolism of medieval alchemy. Ostensibly the alchemists were dabblers in a very rudimentary and superstitious form of chemistry in the hope of being able to turn lead into gold. But it seems that this was merely a mask or front for a strictly spiritual work — the transformation of humanity into divinity. The external trappings of the alchemist — his retorts, furnaces, salts, and metals — were symbols that would inform the initiated and mislead the profane, and especially those who might want to persecute alchemists for supposedly unorthodox religious beliefs.

According to alchemical manuscripts that have been handed down to us, the Great Work of transforming the earthly lead into the heavenly gold is to be carried out in an egg-shaped vessel called the *aludel*. This is placed within the incubatory furnace or *athanor*, and in due course the *aludel* "hatches" the Philosopher's Stone which changes lead into gold at a touch. The symbolic drawings in alchemical writings show us the *aludel* surmounted, as in Hindu symbolism, by a mysterious bird which seems to be a mixture of phoenix, gander, and pelican. The latter, it should be noted, is also associated with Christ because of the folk belief that the pelican feeds its young with its own blood.

> *Pelican of mercy, Jesu, Lord and God,*
> *Cleanse me, retched sinner, in thy precious Blood;*
> *Blood, whereof one drop for human kind outpoured,*
> *Might from all transgression have the world restored.*
> — St. Thomas Aquinas

It is interesting that, although the account of the creation of the world in the Bible does not mention the World-Egg, it says that before the universe was formed "the Spirit of God moved upon [more correctly, *brooded over*] the face of the waters," and it is well known that the chief symbol of the Spirit of God is the dove. Furthermore, the Genesis story goes on to tell how God made a space for the world in the waters of chaos by dividing the upper and lower waters with a vault or firmament, which would correspond with the upper half of the Eggshell in other mythologies.

In modern American folklore, however, the Easter egg is the production not of some mystical bird but of a rabbit or hare — a tradition brought to this continent from Central and Western Europe. Familiar as the Easter Bunny now is, his beginnings are almost completely lost, and students of the history of folklore can give us little more information about him than their own guesses. It has been said that this hare was once a bird whom Eostre, the Anglo-Saxon dawn goddess, changed into a four-footed creature. It is easily possible that hare or rabbit may have been a symbol of fertility, rabbits being notably prolific. He may also be connected with the corn spirit, because in many parts of Europe the last sheaf of corn to be cut is called the hare, and the cutting is sometimes called "cutting the tail of the hare." An Easter hare hunt was observed in parts of England from quite early times, and in Hungary and South Germany it has long been the custom for children to put the effigy of a hare in the basket prepared for the Easter eggs. But the origins of the custom are lost in mystery.

Innumerable European folk customs are found, since the fifteenth century, in connection with the Easter Egg. Sometimes the eggs are left white, sometimes they are dyed in plain colors. In parts of Eastern Europe and the Balkan countries they are elaborately painted with symbols, often of crosses and swastikas. In France it has been the custom for children making their first confessions on Holy Saturday to take a present of eggs for the priest, and in some localities children hunt for eggs in the garden. These eggs are said to have been dropped by the church bells, which, silent since Maundy Thursday, have been on a visit to Rome to see the Pope.

Eggs laid on Good Friday are credited with miraculous powers. There is the belief that if such an egg is kept for a hundred years its yolk will turn into a diamond, or that if it is cooked on Easter Sunday it will work as a powerful amulet against sudden death or as a charm for fruitful trees and crops.

All over Europe, Easter is a time for games with eggs. Hard-boiled eggs are rolled at each other on a field, and the one remaining unbroken at the end of the game is called the victor egg. There are villages where, on the Sunday after Easter, everyone takes an egg to the market square and throws it into the air. Whoever fails to catch his egg as it comes down "loses face" with the community and has to pay a forfeit. In many French towns the egg game was that which a plentiful supply of eggs would naturally suggest to the "perennial small boy" — a street battle with eggs as missiles.

With the advent of the industrial era, the Easter egg has been transformed into chocolate and sugar and tinsel, into brilliant cardboard covers for candy, and into luscious-looking but inedible contraptions with windows, giving views of miniature scenery within. Yet, though its presence with us is no more than a convention, and whether it be plain or colored, common hen's egg or confectioner's concoction, whether wrapped in tinfoil or with real gold and jewels (as was once the custom among the wealthy in Czarist Russia), or whether it be regarded as the production of fabulous bird or improbable rabbit — it remains a symbol of the most remote beginnings, of our universe before heaven and earth and time were born.

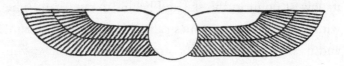

3

SPRING AND
THE SUN CYCLE

The date of Easter is timed from the vernal equinox, that is, from the beginning of spring, when, after the long nights of winter, day and night are equal again before the lengthening days of summer. For there is an annual "journey" of the sun, corresponding to its daily journey from noon to noon through sunset, night, and dawn. In the annual journey, noon corresponds to the summer solstice, when the sun is at its highest point in the sky. Sunset corresponds to the autumnal equinox, when day and night are once again equal before winter, and midnight corresponds to the winter solstice, when the sun reaches its lowest point in the sky and begins to rise again. The winter solstice is sometimes called the Birth of the Sun, and its date is close to Christmas. Dawn, of course, will correspond to the vernal equinox, so that there is always a connection between sunrise and spring.

Indeed, we are told by an ancient English chronicler, the Venerable Bede, that the word "Easter" was originally the name of an Anglo-Saxon goddess of the dawn, known as Eostre or Ostara, whose principal festival was kept at the vernal equinox. We only have Bede's word for it, for no record of such a goddess is to be found elsewhere, but it is unlikely that Bede, as a devout Christian, would have gone out of his way to invent a pagan origin for Easter. But whether or not there was ever such a goddess, it seems most likely that some historical connection must exist between the words "Easter" and "East," where the sun rises.

The date of Easter does not actually coincide with March 22, the vernal equinox, because it changes every year, and may indeed come at any time between March 22 and April 25. The reason for the changing date is not only that Easter Day must always be a Sunday, since Christ rose on the first day of the week, but also that it is determined by both the solar and the lunar calendars. Easter Day is the Sunday following the first full moon after the vernal equinox.

The lunar calendar is brought in together with the solar because, at the time of Christ, the Jews measured their months by the moon, and tradition tells us that Christ was crucified and rose from the dead during the month of Nisan, when the Jews keep the Feast of the Passover. Nisan falls approximately between March 22 and April 22. Thus the Latin and Greek word for Easter is *Pascha*, which is simply a form of the Hebrew word for Passover — *Pesach*.

If we look at the accompanying diagram, we shall see that there is a suggestive correspondence between the Christ story and at least one half of the annual and daily journeys of the sun — the ascending half. It has already been noted that Christmas, the Birth of Christ, observed by tradition on December 25, coincides almost exactly with the winter solstice, the Birth of the Sun, and there is a further tradition that Christ was born at midnight.

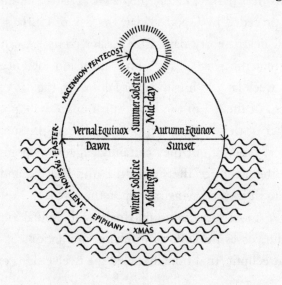

Following the Christ story as it is commemorated in the Christian Year, we find that the next important feast is Epiphany, the feast of the Manifestation of Christ's Glory to the nations, typified in the Three Kings who followed the Star of Bethlehem to the place of his birth and made their offerings of gold, frankincense, and myrrh. Thus there is a traditional symbolic connection between Christ and the Morning Star, the name given to any bright star or planet, such as Venus, which rises after midnight. After Epiphany comes Lent, the season of fasting, which is at once a memorial of Christ's own forty-day fast in the wilderness and a convenient means of conserving the dwindling supplies of food toward the end of winter.

Lent ends with Easter, corresponding to dawn and spring, and, as "it is darkest before the dawn," Easter is immediately preceded by Good Friday, the day of Christ's sacrificial death. Forty days after Easter comes Ascension Day, remembering Christ's final ascension into heaven, and a week later Whitsunday or Pentecost, the day of the descent of the fire of the Holy Spirit upon the Apostles. Neither of these feasts ever come as late as the summer solstice, June 22, but they certainly suggest or point toward the ascent of the sun to the mid-heaven, and the descent of its life-giving rays upon the earth.

We know, too, that in making its full annual journey the sun passes through the twelve constellations of stars on the ecliptic, traditionally called the twelve signs of the

Zodiac, and Christian imagination has seen a resemblance between the sun and its twelve signs and Christ and his twelve disciples. Indeed the ancient symbols for the four authors of the Gospels are the four so-called "fixed signs of the Zodiac" — the Man (Aquarius) for Matthew, the Lion (Leo) for Mark, the Bull (Taurus) for Luke, and the Eagle or Phoenix (an alternative symbol for Scorpio) for John. Of course, neither Mark nor Luke were among the original twelve disciples, but the language of symbols is never anything more than suggestive, and it invariably takes a wide range of "poetic license" with literal and historical accuracy.

That quarter of the sun's journey which lies between the vernal equinox and the summer solstice has, from the most ancient times, been a season of religious rites connected with the sowing and the fruition of crops. We have already pointed to the parallel, suggested by Christ himself, between his death and resurrection and the planting and sprouting of the grain of corn. It may also be remembered that he likened himself to the vine, and ordained that wine, the "blood" of the crushed grape, should be the sacramental vehicle of his own blood in the celebration of the Lord's Supper or Eucharist. The fact that bread is made from ground corn and wine from crushed grapes has long been connected in religious symbolism with the idea that eternal as well as material life is the result of sacrifice — of life-giving death. It is probable, then, that the Christian Easter has absorbed many of the ancient rites and observances associated, not only with the sun, but also with the fertility of the soil.

Whereas the ascent of the sun is connected with the world's salvation, mythology connects its descending journey with creation. Many stories relate that at sunset the sun descends into those mysterious waters of chaos out of which the universe was created, and in the midst of which the World-Egg floats. Indeed, the world first came out of the waters because the divine Spirit, symbolized by the sun, descended into them and brought order and life out of chaos. The universe is the Spirit expressing itself through matter, through material, which is of the same root as the word "maternal," so that myth almost universally equates the primeval waters with the Universal Mother Goddess in whose womb the world is formed by the action of the Spirit.

Such ideas survive in Christian symbolism. Christ himself is conceived by the Holy Spirit and born of the Virgin Mother of God. The Christian is initiated or "born again" in baptism with water and the Spirit, and on Easter Eve the priest blesses the waters of the baptismal font by plunging the lighted Paschal Candle into their depths. The very prayer accompanying this act likens the waters of the font to the chaos-waters over which the Spirit brooded in the beginning of time.

Thus creation, the descent of the sun into the waters, is the entry of Spirit into the material womb, wherein it lies hidden and awaiting its awakening. The Genesis story says that God formed man out of the material dust, and breathed his own Spirit into the man's nostrils. Salvation, the ascent of the sun, is the awakening of Spirit within the Mother, the manifesting of God in man as distinct from the original concealment of God in man.

Probably the greatest of the ancient sun gods was the Egyptian Ra. One of our best sources of information about him is the world's oldest book on death and resurrection, the so-called *Book of the Dead*, whose true title is *The Book of Coming Forth by Day*. The book opens with a number of "Hymns to Ra when he Riseth," wherein so plain a connection is made between the rising of the sun and the resurrection of the soul from death that they might well be called the first Easter hymns.

> Hail, thou Disk, thou lord of rays, who risest on the horizon day by day! Shine thou with thy beams of light upon the face of [thy servant], who is victorious, for he singeth hymns of praise unto thee at dawn.... May the soul of [thy servant], the triumphant one, come forth with thee into heaven....
>
> May I not be shut up [in the tomb], may I not be turned back, may the limbs of my body be made new again when I view thy beauties,... because I am one of those who worshiped thee upon earth. May I come in unto the land of eternity, may I come even unto the everlasting land,

for behold, O my lord, this thou hast ordained
for me.

The hymns dwell, too, on the theme of the Sun Spirit
awakening within Nut, the Universal Mother, the "wa-
tery mass out of which all the gods were evolved."

Thou risest, thou shinest, thou makest light in
thy mother; thou art crowned king of the gods.
Thy mother Nut doeth an act of homage unto
thee with both her hands.

The hymns likewise describe the sun journey, telling how he ascends in the Atet boat and descends in the
Sektet boat, accompanied by the two fishes, Abtu and
Ant, with Thoth, the personification of divine wisdom,
sitting in the prow and keeping the boats on their course.
At sunset he descends at the mountain called Manu into
the underworld and there engages in battle with the serpent Apep, ever lying in wait to devour the sun. But Apep
is destroyed and hewn in pieces.

In the Babylonian version of the myth the sun
god is Marduk and the serpent of darkness is Tiamat,
and when Tiamat is slain Marduk splits her in two parts,
the upper making the vault of heaven and the lower the
floor of earth. Man is then created in the space between.
Both stories suggest a connection between the sun's
descent and the act of creation, for creation is repeat-
edly figured as a victory over the serpent or dragon of

darkness and chaos. Moreover, it may not be altogether fanciful to associate the mountain Manu at, or into, which Ra descends at sunset with the *Manu*, or primordial man, of Hindu myth — from which comes our own word "man." Likewise, the underworld into which Ra descends at evening is not merely the place of departed souls. The mythical underworld is in some sense *this* world, which has been created out of the body of the dragon.

In comparison with the eternal and divine world, this material world is indeed both "under" and "dark" because for the majority of men the divine Spirit within them is forgotten; it is in the darkness of the unconscious; the true nature of their inmost being is unknown. The greatest enigma of man's life is the problem of who or what he really is — what is that mysterious center in him which knows, that light of the mind called consciousness. The "blind spot" in the soul is the very place from which we see. The language of myth is ever suggesting that this "blind spot" from which the light of the mind originates is the Spiritual Sun who has descended into those dark waters which represent not only chaos but also the unconscious depths of man's psychology. In the words of St. John's Gospel, the Divine Being is "the true light which enlightens every man that cometh into the world." But when, at evening, the sun descends into "the waters beneath the earth," into *materia*, Mother Nature, it becomes unknown. In bringing all the multitude of forms and creatures into being, the Creator remains invisible and hidden.*

In him was life; and the life was the light of men.
And the light shineth in darkness; and the darkness
  comprehended it not....
He was in the world, and the world was made by him,
  and the world knew him not.

But the Spiritual Sun is hidden not because it is remote but because it rests in the central "blind spot." As the proverb says, "The nearer to the lamp, the darker the shadow." And likewise the mystic, "God is nearer to me than I am to myself."

Though we find all kinds of resemblances between the Christ story on the one hand, and, on the other, the motions of the sun, the growth of corn and vine, and the myths of gods who were ancient when Christ was born, we are not suggesting that the Christ story is some mere survival of old superstitions tacked on to the true history of a Galilean prophet. Such resemblances were well known to the early Christians, and to the Christian mind they are but further evidence for the divinity of Jesus. For Christianity sees him as the embodiment or incarnation of the *Word* of God. This Word means the ideal pattern or divine law by which, and in accordance with which,

---

* It is only when the sun goes down that the universe of stars appears.

the universe and man are created. If, then, the Word is the design in the mind of the Architect of the Universe, there will be every reason to expect resemblances between the life of Christ and all the processes of nature as they are found in the heavens, in man, and in the life of the soil. This, then, is why Christ rises from the dead with the ascending sun, and at the season when the crops rise from the ground. For the works of the Maker are all of a piece, and behind Christ and crops and seasons and the inner workings of the human mind is one spirit, one rhythm, one moving pulse.

"The very thing that is now called the Christian religion," wrote St. Augustine, "was not wanting among the ancients from the beginning of the human race, until Christ came in the flesh, after which the true religion, which had already existed, began to be called 'Christian.'"

THE RESURRECTION

Modern Indian *(Artist unknown)*

4

THE GODS
WHO DIED AND ROSE

Nearly seven thousand years ago, a people called the Sumerians lived beyond Arabia in the valley of the river Euphrates. Today the river winds its way through desert sands, for wind, neglect, and soil erosion have long since wiped out the gardens of olive and cypress, of date palms and spice trees, which were once the life of the valley where the civilization of the Near East was born. Ruins only mark the sites of Ur and Babylon, fabulous cities of wealth and luxury, where astronomy, mathematics, and writing were practiced when Egypt itself was young.

From these incredibly remote times there comes the story of Tammuz, a god whose name means "true son of the deep waters" — a name suggestive not only of the World-Egg which the Divine Bird laid in the primordial ocean but also of the Christian principle that no one is a true son of God unless, in baptism, he is born of water and the Spirit.

Wife and beloved of Tammuz was the goddess Inanna, or Ishtar, in whose person is represented she whom we now call Mother Nature or Mother Earth — she who, when refreshed with the spring rains, with the water from heaven, brings forth the fruits of life. We are told that when Tammuz died, Inanna was so stricken with grief that she followed him to the underworld, to the realm of Eresh-Kigal, Queen of the Dead, a "land from which there is no returning, a house of darkness, where dust lies on door and bolt." In her absence the earth was deprived of its fertility; crops would not grow; animals would not mate; life was in danger of coming to an end.

> *"O my child!" at his vanishing away she lifts up a*
> *lament;*
> *"My Damu!" at his vanishing away she lifts up a*
> *lament;*
> *"My enchanter and priest!" at his vanishing away*
> *she lifts up a lament,*

At the shining cedar, rooted in a spacious place,
In Eanna, above and below, she lifts up a lament.

So an ancient text, called *The Lament of the Flutes for Tammuz*, describes the grief which moved Ea, god of water and wisdom, to send a heavenly messenger to the underworld to rescue the goddess whose absence was removing life from the earth. Assenting reluctantly to his supreme will, Eresh-Kigal allowed the messenger to sprinkle Inanna and Tammuz with the water of life — a potion which gave them power to return into the light of the sun for six months of the year. But for the other six months, Tammuz must again return to the land of death, whither Inanna would again pursue him, and once more with her lamentations move Ea to give the water of life so that year after year the miracle of resurrection and spring would recur.

In the course of centuries, the story and the yearly rites connected with the death and resurrection of Tammuz moved westward to Phoenicia and Syria on the extreme east of the Mediterranean. Here the name of Tammuz was changed to Adon or Adonai, meaning "the lord," and the name of Inanna (or Ishtar) to Astarte. In Greek the two names are Adonis and Aphrodite, and it is from Greek writers that we know most about the myth of Adon and of the changes which it underwent in passing from Sumeria to Syria.

They tell us that Adonis was the child of Myrrha, the myrtle tree, and it seems that almost all the gods of death and resurrection are associated with a tree — Tammuz with the tamarisk and willow, Osiris and Attis with the pine, and Christ himself with the Tree of the Cross. When the infant Adonis was born, Aphrodite was so charmed with his beauty that she adopted him and concealed him in a chest, which she gave for safe-keeping to Persephone, who is the counterpart of Eresh-Kigal, Queen of the Dead. (The theme of the mother who "loves her child to death" is as old as the world.) In the underworld Persephone opened the chest, and was herself so enchanted with the babe that she decided to keep him. This led to a dispute between Aphrodite and Persephone, between love and death, in which Zeus (taking the place of Ea) had to intervene. Zeus decreed that for four months of the year Adonis should belong to Aphrodite, for four to Persephone, and for the remaining four he should do as he wished — whereupon Adonis chose to spend them with Aphrodite.

When he had grown to young manhood, Adonis roused the envy of Artemis, the forest goddess of the hunt, or, according to another account, of Ares, the god of war. Thus, while he was out hunting, Artemis slew Adonis with an arrow — the arrows of Artemis being the cause to which sudden death was generally ascribed — or, in the other version, he was gored by Ares in the form of a wild boar. He died, and where the earth had received his blood, Aphrodite sprinkled the ground with nectar, so that the blood turned into anemones and other flowers of the field. But the grief of Aphrodite was so piteous that the gods of the underworld allowed Adonis to return to her every spring for six months of the year.

In Asia Minor, among the people of the Phrygian Hills, Adonis went by the name of Attis, and his spouse-mother Aphrodite was called Cybele, Rhea, or Dindymene. Attis was the supernatural son of Nana, a virgin who had eaten the fruit of an almond tree which, in turn, had grown up from the blood of the dismembered Agdistis, a god both male and female who was the offspring of Zeus and Ge (the Earth). Cybele was the Great Mother of All the Gods, daughter of Earth (Ge) and Sky (Uranus). Zeus himself was her son, as were also Pluto, lord of the underworld, and Poseidon, lord of waters.

Now Cybele was in love with Attis, but he himself wished to marry another, the daughter of the king of Pessinus. However, the Great Mother Goddess sent him out of his mind with her magical powers so that he mutilated himself and died beneath a pine tree. From his blood sprang, not anemones but violets, and by another miracle of her divine power the goddess brought about his resurrection from the pine into which his spirit had passed.

Of the same essential pattern is the great Egyptian myth of Osiris, and the story as told by the Greek historian Plutarch is actually connected with the city of Byblos in Syria, which was the center of the Adonis cult. Like

Tammuz, "true son of the deep waters," Osiris is referred to upon an Egyptian monument as "he who springs from the returning waters."

The parents of Osiris are those who brought forth the World-Egg, Geb (the Earth) and Nut (the Sky), who are likewise the parents of his wife and sister Isis, who plays the same part in the Egyptian pantheon as Inanna, Aphrodite, and Cybele — the Great Mother Goddess, most popular of all divinities, who is venerated in every part of the world, in India as Maya-Shakti, Lakshmi, Sita, and Kali, in China as Kwan-yin, goddess of mercy, and whose cult effectually lives on in Catholic devotion to Mary, Queen of Heaven and Mother of God.

The story goes that Set, the Evil One, conspired against Osiris for the rule of his kingdom. By stealth, Set obtained the exact measurements of Osiris' body and fashioned an exquisite casket into which that body alone would fit. So beautiful was the casket that when Set and his henchmen brought it into the palace of Osiris, everyone present desired to own it and began to demand its price. Set replied that it should belong to him whose body it fitted, and one by one the members of the company attempted to lie down in the casket. But none of them fitted. In the end, Osiris himself was persuaded to lie down, and at that instant Set slammed the lid and sealed it with molten lead. Immediately thereafter, Set bore the casket away and threw it into the river Nile, whence it drifted out to sea.

Like Inanna, Isis began to lament and to search for her beloved. In due course, she learned that the casket had been carried by the sea to Byblos, where, on being washed ashore, it had grown up into an immense tamarisk, or pine tree, whose splendid trunk had so impressed the king of Byblos that he had ordered it cut down and made the central pillar of his palace.

Journeying to Byblos, Isis revealed her identity to the king and queen and procured the casket with the dead Osiris from inside the great trunk of the tree. But shortly after she had brought it back to Egypt, the casket was found by Set, who, in his rage, tore open the lid and sundered the body of Osiris into fourteen pieces which he scattered up and down the length of Egypt.

Once more Isis set out to retrieve the body. Some accounts say that wherever she found one of the pieces she buried it and built a shrine in her beloved's honor. Other accounts say that she gathered the pieces together in a corn sieve, and, with the aid of Thoth, the god of wisdom, and Horus, her son by Osiris, brought the dismembered body back to life. However, Egyptian pictures of the resurrection of Osiris show him emerging from a sarcophagus or from a broken egg, with Thoth, Horus, Isis, Anubis, and other divine personages performing magical rites about the bier.

Risen from death, Osiris became the lord of the Tuat, or underworld, and the judge of the living and the dead, entitled he who is "Eternity and Everlastingness," who, in the fullness of time, should come again to reign upon earth. The parallel with the Christian creed is obvious, save that the Egyptian paradise is regarded as below rather than above. "And he shall come again with glory to judge both the living and the dead; whose kingdom shall have no end."

In the temple of Isis whose ruins remain at Philae in Egypt, the body of Osiris is shown lying upon the ground with grain stalks growing up from it. In the mysteries of Osiris celebrated at Denderah, his ritual effigies were made in a mold from a paste of wheat flour. Together with the anecdote of his resurrection from a corn sieve, this connects his myth not only with the symbolism of vegetation and bread but also with the symbolism of Christianity, where the risen Christ lives on not only in heaven but also in the sacramental Bread of the Mass. And as the body of Osiris was cut in pieces and the fructifying blood of Adonis spilled on the ground, so in the Christian mystery the Holy Bread of Christ's Body is broken for communion, and the Wine of his Blood poured out for the giving of eternal life.

One of the earliest accounts of Christian worship, a book called the *Didache*, gives us the prayer which the first Christians used at the breaking of bread: "We give thanks unto thee, our Father, for the life and knowledge which thou didst make known unto us through Jesus thy servant....As this broken bread was scattered upon the tops of the hills and being gathered became one, so gather thy Church [which is Christ's 'Mystical Body'] from the ends of the earth into thy Kingdom."

Substantially the same theme appears in the Greek myth of Demeter and Kore (Persephone), which was associated with the famous Mysteries of Eleusis. Eleusis, near Athens, was the scene of one of the greatest religious mystery rites in the ancient world (a subject to which we shall return in the next chapter), and many of the most important writers and philosophers of Greece and Rome bore witness to their ennobling effects.

Demeter, like Inanna, Isis, and Cybele, is once again the embodiment of the Great Mother, but this time the story is concerned not with her lover but with her daughter, Kore. The girl was abducted by Pluto, the ruler of the underworld, and her absence brought about a famine on earth through the failure of the crops. Pluto was therefore moved to restore Kore to her mother, but because she had eaten a pomegranate in the underworld she was bound to return to Pluto for as many months of each year as there were seeds of the pomegranate caught in her mouth. In joy at her annual return, the earth (Demeter) brings forth her fruits and flowers.

Ancient Greece had other mystery religions besides those practiced at Eleusis. Of special importance were the Bacchic and Orphic mysteries, both of which were concerned with the myth of Dionysus, god of the vine. Whereas the Bacchic mysteries too often assumed the form of drunken revels, the Orphic rites were introduced as a reform and were ennobled by a lofty theology and morality.

Like Osiris, Dionysus was born of earth and sky, his father being Zeus, the lord of heaven, and his mother Semele, whose name denotes the earth, as does her nature. For she was human, the daughter of Cadmus of Thebes, and thus Dionysus was called *dithyrhambus*, meaning he who enters life by a "double door," both human and divine. It is not in this alone that he is similar to Christ, conceived of the Spirit and born of woman, and declared to be at once true God and true man. We have said that Dionysus was the vine god. His special symbols were the grape cluster, the drinking cup or chalice, and wine itself, and in his rites he was held actually to *become* the wine poured out in his honor. We have already called attention to Christ's description of himself as the vine, and in Catholic doctrine the consecrated wine of the altar actually becomes his Blood.

In one important respect, however, the story of Dionysus differs from those of Tammuz, Adonis, Osiris, and Kore. For his very birth was his resurrection. He had existed in a prior state as Zagreus, the son of Zeus and Persephone, a son so favored of Zeus that he had been allowed to sit on the throne of heaven and wield his father's lightnings. But this inspired the jealousy and rage of the Titans, the primeval giants, who lured the child away by stealth and tore him in pieces as Set had dismembered Osiris. On discovering this, Zeus destroyed the Titans with lightning, and from their ashes created the race of men. In the meantime he preserved and swallowed the heart of Zagreus, and this heart became Dionysus the son of Zeus and Semele.

The fact that mankind had been created from the ashes of Titans who had both dismembered and eaten Dionysus-Zagreus was used in Orphic theology as an allegory for the divine origin of man. The substance of Dionysus had entered the Titans, and thus was contained in their ashes, so that it passed in turn into the substance of man. "The body," said Olympiodorus, "is not to be destroyed because it is one with Dionysus." This kind of "double resurrection" or resurrection-and-transformation has its parallel in Christianity, too. For Christ at once rises entire from the dead and at the same time is broken and eaten sacramentally in the Mass, so that his "substance" enters the worshipers, making them his Mystical Body "which is the blessed company of all faithful people."

The common elements in all these stories are so apparent that one may think of them as a single drama performed again and again by different actors. The god dies by descending to the underworld as the seed is sown in the dark earth, or by dismemberment as the ear of corn is broken up and scattered over the fields. And as, with the coming of spring, the scattered and buried grain rises young and green into the light and, on ripening, is gathered and united into the one Bread which is the source of our life, so the dead god rises at the vernal equinox to become the source of eternal life for those initiated into his "mystery."

THE CRUCIFIXION

Alan Watts

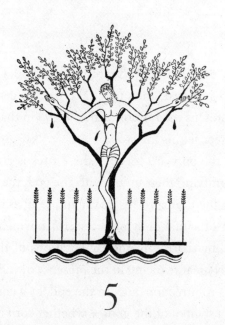

5

THE ANCIENT MYSTERIES

In connection with each one of the stories of the gods which we have told, there was something which the ancient world called a Mystery. In brief, a Mystery is a kind of secret society which enjoys union with its god, a group of persons who share his divine and eternal life. Membership in the Mystery is open to chosen individuals, who, after special tests of their fitness, usually undergo an initiation which represents their death as individuals and their resurrection in the form of the god. Once they have been initiated, they may take part in certain rites which represent their union with the god in that the participants reenact his life story.

Thus the outward form of these rites is always dramatic. Signifying their union with the god, the worshipers repeat the drama of his death and resurrection — by some sort of actual or symbolic sacrifice which refers to his death, by sharing in the lamentations of the Earth-Mother, by great rejoicing in the presence of various symbols of his resurrection, and, in the end, by a communion in which a symbol of the god — whether corn or wine or sacrificial animal — is eaten by his devotees. For a man is what he eats. To become one with his god, he eats him. The idea may be naive, but it is extraordinarily graphic.

We know a great deal about the Christian Mystery, but our knowledge of the older Mysteries is very limited for the reason that their initiates kept the vows of secrecy most rigidly. There was a time when the Christian Mystery was also a secret, when only baptized persons were admitted to the inner rites of the Church. But when the whole Roman Empire and the European peoples at large were supposedly "converted" to Christianity, its Mystery became public property; for the public was a Christian public.

No one who knows anything of the ancient Mystery cults can fail to recognize that the full form of the Christian Holy Week and Easter rites is a Mystery — a tremendous drama of the Christian's union with Christ in his passion, death, and resurrection. Unhappily there are now few Christians who ever see the full enactment of this drama because — in our modern sophistication — we have become stuffy and stodgy and given to religious observances which are both brief and dull, and in which the people have little or no active part. Originally, all worship was an action — a thing done, not a thing said — and words were only employed to indicate the meaning of the action.*

It is perhaps true that in the earliest beginnings of ancient civilization these Mysteries were a form of "sympathetic magic." Their object was possibly to encourage the growing of the crops by a sign language reminding the corn spirit to rise from his annual slumber. As we shall see, it is true that, even today, various Easter observances are regarded by European peasants as helpful to the fertility of their fields. But it is also possible that the merely magical understanding of myth and Mystery is degenerate rather than original. It is likewise possible that, in the most far-off and primitive times, these rites were a type of "play" for which men had no more conscious reason or explanation than a bird has for singing. It is certain, however, that at the (quite early) times when

---

* It is only in relatively late times that Christians have talked of worship as "hearing Mass," or worse, "going to hear Dr. So-and-So." The truly traditional Christian would speak of going to "*assist* at Mass," or better, of going to "*make*" or "*do* the Liturgy." Liturgy, an old word for the Church service, means literally the "public work."

these rites were Mysteries in the sense described, their main point was to signify a union between the performers and the god. Ancient literature leaves us in no doubt on this.

Golden tablets of the Orphic Mysteries discovered in tombs at Sybaris carry inscriptions in which the initiated soul proclaims, "I am the Son of Earth and Heaven"; and again, "O blessed and happy one, thou hast put off thy mortality and shalt become divine." According to the Latin writer, Sallust, "The intention of all mystic ceremonies is to conjoin us with the world and the gods." In even stronger terms the Egyptian *Book of the Dead* has the initiate saying, "I am the divine Soul of Ra proceeding from the god Nu; that divine soul which is God....I am the god Nu...I am the first-born god of primeval matter, that is to say, the divine Soul, even the Souls of the gods of everlastingness, and my body is eternity." Likewise the Catholic Mass contains the prayer that Christ "who vouchsafed to partake of our humanity, may make us partakers of his divinity."

It would be tedious to describe in detail all that has been handed down to us about the various rites of Tammuz, Adonis, Kore, Dionysus, and many others, for their rites had as many basic elements in common as their respective myths. Some of them were celebrated at the vernal equinox, or thereabouts, and some at midsummer. But their universal theme — the drama of death and resurrection — makes them the forerunners of the Christian Easter, and thus the first "Easter services." As we go on to describe the Christian observance of Easter we shall see how many of its customs and ceremonies resemble these former rites. For the moment it will be of interest to look at two of them in particular.

The first is a very ancient rite that came to Rome from the East two hundred years before Christ — a rite whose external details are believed to have had some influence on Christian ceremonial. We have already told the story of Cybele and Attis, a form of the Inanna-Tammuz and Aphrodite-Adonis cult which seems to have been developed in Asia Minor. The celebrations in their honor which we are about to describe would have taken place in a many-pillared temple on one of the seven hills of Rome, perhaps in the year 100 BCE.

Shortly before the vernal equinox — to be exact, on the Ides, or fifteenth day, of March — the members of this cult began a fast — as Christians also have the fast of Lent, beginning forty days before Easter. On the second day of this fast, a group of young men would gather together for an expedition to a nearby forest. These men, doubtless young priests of the goddess, were known as Dendrophori or Tree-bearers, and when they reached the forest they sought out a great and noble pine tree, for it was under a pine that Attis was said to have died. Cutting the tree down, the Tree-bearers carried it with reverence and ceremony to Cybele's temple and set it up in the central sanctuary. Here, like a Christmas tree, it was decorated with various ornaments, many-colored strips of ribbon, and especially with festoons of violets — the flower said to have grown from the spilled blood of Attis. Upon its central stem was hung the figure of the young God.

Here, for the remaining days of the fast, the worshipers gathered to sing hymns of mourning for the dead Attis — wild, plaintive songs, whose cadences may still be heard in the folk music of Greece and Asia Minor, of the Phrygian Hills in which the Mystery of Cybele had its home. And to this day, on Good Friday at the Veneration of the Cross, Christians sing their hymn of mourning for another and greater one who died on a Tree:

> Bend thy boughs, O Tree of glory,
>   Thy relaxing sinews bend:
> For a while the ancient rigor
>   That thy birth bestowed, suspend:*
> And the King of heavenly beauty
>   On thy bosom gently tend.

Nine days later, on March 24, came the Day of Blood. Wrong and repulsive as the worship of this day may seem

---

* There is a legend that the Cross on which Christ was crucified was made from a beam grown from a cutting from the very Tree of Knowledge, the eating of whose fruit had caused the Fall of Adam. Thus the "ancient rigor" is presumably the subjection of man to death as a result of the Fall.

in comparison with the sublimity of Good Friday, it none-theless embodies the same theme of union with divinity through self-sacrifice. Gathered before the great tree in the temple, the worshipers, stripped naked to the waist, knives in hand, began a fantastic and abandoned dance to the accompaniment of a frantic music of pipes and drums.

With the growing passion and madness of the music, the dancers started to whirl and spin "so that their hair flew out in a circle." In the extreme of excitement they bit their own flesh and, slashing themselves with the knives, sprinkled the sacred tree with their blood. But in the ultimate spasm of frenzy and self-abandonment to the goddess, imitating the madness of Attis, young men would rush to the tree and make themselves eunuchs — in the firm conviction that this terrible sacrifice of their manhood made them one with Attis, and partakers of his immortality. Such men thereafter became the priests and initiates of the Mystery.*

Sometimes the Day of Blood was also the occasion of the *taurobolium*, or bull sacrifice, for the gods of death and resurrection were associated not only with plants and trees but also with certain animals — Mithra and Attis with the bull, Dionysus with the goat, and Christ himself with the lamb. At the *taurobolium* a bull, richly decorated with gold and flowers, was slain with a ritual

---

* Is it possible that Jesus had such men in mind when he said there "there are eunuchs who have made themselves eunuchs for the kingdom of heaven's sake"? (Matthew 19:12)

spear, and those upon whom the blood was poured were venerated as Attis himself. One is reminded inevitably of the Christian Easter hymn in the Breviary:

> *The Lamb's high banquet we await*
> *In snow-white robes of royal state....*
> *Upon the Altar of the Cross*
> *His Body hath redeemed our loss:*
> *And tasting of his roseate Blood,*
> *Our life is hid with him in God.*

Likewise in the Mass of the Orthodox Church, the sacred Bread for consecration is cut with a knife shaped like a spear, while the priest says, "He was led as a sheep to the slaughter; and as a spotless lamb before his shearers is dumb, so opened he not his mouth."

As the Day of Blood drew to its close, the figure of the dead Attis was taken down from the tree and buried under the twilight sky. Far into the night his devotees stood around the grave and sang hymns of mourning. But as dawn approached, a great light was kindled, as today Christians light the Paschal Candle on Easter Eve as a symbol of the risen Christ. Describing the final scene, an eyewitness wrote: "When they are satisfied with their feigned grief a light is brought in, and the priest, having anointed their lips, whispers, 'Be of good cheer, you of the Mystery. Your god is saved; for us also there shall be salvation from ills.'"

Thus began the day of March 25, a day of unbounded rejoicing and festivity in honor of the resurrection of Attis, a day called the *Hilaria* — from which we get our word "hilarity."

The rites that we have described not only celebrated the death and resurrection of Attis; they were also the occasion for initiation into the Mystery. In the light of Christianity we do not find the means of initiation at all edifying, and there were many other Mysteries in which the act of death to one's former self was not thus brutally and crudely symbolized. Yet all Mysteries have the common idea that initiation into the divine life of the god comes about through "dying" with him. St. Paul described Christian initiation — the sacrament of baptism — as being "baptized into Christ's death," and for this reason Easter Eve, the day of Christ's lying in the tomb, used to be the normal and proper time for all baptisms.

Something much closer to Christian initiation than the bloody rite of Attis may be found in the Mystery of Isis and Osiris. Our description of these rites dates from a late period of Egyptian history, when Greek kings ruled in the place of the ancient pharaohs. Of the early Mysteries of Osiris we have only fragmentary accounts, as of the Mysteries at Denderah, held in the month of Khoiak, the beginning of the Egyptian spring. Here an effigy of Osiris, made of a paste of wheat flour, was fashioned about the twelfth day of the month, dried in the sun, and transported in a royal barge along the Nile to the place of the tombs. On the twenty-fifth day of the month the effigy was buried in a tomb specially set apart. Representing the various divinities who brought Osiris back to life — Thoth, Isis, Horus, and Anubis — the priests conducted the rites of resurrection over the buried image.

In the later development of the Mystery, with which we are concerned here, the candidate for initiation took the place of the effigy, for the crux of the rite was a ceremonial burial. The Mystery began with a fast — just as the Christian catechumens, or candidates for baptism, kept a very special fast during the Lent and Holy Week prior to their initiation. After this, the neophyte, as one undergoing initiation is called, was baptized in waters taken from the sacred Nile, Egypt's river of life and fertility — as Christians are sometimes baptized in water from the Jordan.

Sometimes this baptism was held in the Nile itself, along whose red banks stand most of the great temples of Egypt, and we can picture the neophyte being led up from the river, up the white marble steps flanked with crouching lions hewn of black basalt, and in through the long colonnade of painted pillars with lotus-like capitals. Before the vast door of the sanctuary, carved and painted with the animal-headed symbols of divinity, the neophyte passed through the ranks of priests with shaven heads and leopard skins thrown across their shoulders — passed through the door into the inmost shrine. Here, in the incense-laden darkness of the sanctuary, he was laid upon a bier, or perhaps in a sarcophagus, and over his recumbent body the hierophant, that is, the initiating priest, performed funerary rites appropriate to the dead Osiris himself. This included covering the neophyte with the hide of a cow, the animal sacred to Isis the Earth-Mother, typifying thus his burial in the earth.

Thereafter the hierophant took an adze in his hands and with it touched the neophyte upon the nose, the mouth, the eyes, and other members of the body, calling them to life with the very instrument of death which had been used for the dismemberment of Osiris.* So also in the Orthodox Church the newly baptized Christian is immediately anointed with holy oil upon the brow, the eyes, nostrils, lips, ears, hands, and feet, signifying the gift of the Holy Spirit of life.

This done, the neophyte was helped to his feet and vested in the robes of Osiris. A lighted taper was put in his hand — as the baptized Christian is given a candle after receiving the white garment of purity — and he was then led to the outer court of the temple, where the people venerated him as Osiris in the flesh. "As truly as Osiris lives," it was proclaimed, "he also shall live. As truly as Osiris is not dead, shall he not die. As truly as Osiris is not annihilated, shall he not be annihilated."

Prepared by many months of instruction and meditation, the neophyte was expected, during these rites, to

---

* So, too, the Christian finds life through the Cross, the instrument of Christ's execution.

have a spiritual experience of his union with the ultimate Reality behind the universe, personified in Osiris. One who passed through the initiation has left us this single enigmatic fragment of explanation: "Understand that I approached the bounds of death; I trod the threshold of Persephone [i.e., the underworld]; and after that I was ravished through all the elements, I returned to my proper place. About midnight I saw the sun brightly shine."

Many other examples of these Mystery rites might be described, and in almost all of them we should find the same basic symbols, the same essential drama. Man acquires the eternal life of the divinity through death, through sharing in the death of the Savior-God. In the words of St. Paul, "I am crucified with Christ; nevertheless, I live: yet not I, but Christ liveth in me."

Once again, let it be said that the devout Christian need feel no disturbance at what may seem crude parodies of the Christ story, and of the splendid worship which the Church offers at Holy Week and Easter. For the Christ story can only find its way into the human heart because a place for it has already been prepared. Distorted, indeed, by the flawed glass of the human mind, the light of the Spirit has been shining through all the ages to show the Way from death to resurrection, from Calvary to the Empty Tomb.

The Christian conviction is simply that in Christ that light shines without distortion. Furthermore, it has elements in common with the rites of the rising sun and the sprouting corn, and with all the pagan worship of Nature, because the story of Christ is the story of Nature's Lord — manifested in the flesh.

The same point was made long ago in the book of the Wisdom of Solomon, which speaks of those who "deemed either fire, or wind, or the swift air, or the circle of the stars, or the violent water, or the lights of heaven, to be the gods which govern the world. With whose beauty if they being delighted took them to be gods, let them know how much better the Lord of them is; for the first author of beauty hath created them.... For by the greatness and beauty of the creatures, proportionately the maker of them is seen."*

---

* From the Apocrypha. Wisdom 13:2–3, 5.

6

THE LAMB OF GOD

One of the most familiar symbols of Easter is the Lamb with the red cross banner. In stained glass, stonework, and embroidery, it is one of the commonest themes of Church art, and references to the lamb in Christian scripture and worship are so frequent that, next to the Cross itself, it is probably the most important symbol of Christianity. Usually the Agnus Dei, or Lamb of God, represents Christ. Sometimes, however, it also stands for the human being, as when Christ is portrayed as the Good Shepherd carrying a lamb upon his shoulders.

The symbol comes from the same source as the word *Pascha*, the Greek and Latin name for Easter, which was originally the Hebrew word *Pesach*, the Feast of the Passover, at which lambs were sacrificed in commemoration of the deliverance of Israel from Egypt some four thousand years ago. For the ancient Hebrews found one of their principal means of livelihood in sheepherding, and it was therefore natural that this important occupation should provide so many of their religious symbols and allegories.

It is also natural that the symbol should be somewhat puzzling to those for whom sheep are of no great importance. It seems that the average modern city dweller regards the sheep as a rather stupid animal. He finds it incongruous as a symbol of Christ, and resents the notion that he himself is one of the sheep of his pastor's congregation. Missionaries, too, have had their difficulties in explaining this symbol in lands where sheep have never been seen. In trying to convert an African tribe where the chief domestic animal was the curly pig, a missionary hit upon the ingenious idea of referring to the Lamb of God as "the Curly Pig of God," and began to talk about being saved "through the Blood of the Curly Pig." Unfortunately this gave the tribe the impression that Christians were a strange group of simpletons who imagined that God was a curly pig, and it was many years before white men and missionaries ceased to be held in ridicule and disrespect.

The Paschal Lamb became a symbol of Christ as the Jewish Passover became the Christian Easter. And as the Passover commemorated the deliverance of the Hebrews from captivity in Egypt, so the Christian mind saw a figurative connection between the bondage of Egypt and the bondage of death, and between the Exodus, or escape from Egypt, and the Resurrection. Here, indeed, is the most immediate relation between the Christian and the pre-Christian story of Easter, for Christ himself and almost all the first Christians were Hebrews.

More than two thousand years before Christ's time — possibly under the rule of Rameses II — a desert tribe of Bedouin nomads had become the serfs of the Egyptian king. This king was a great builder of monuments and other "public works," and the Hebrew tribesmen were put to work chiefly in making bricks and hauling rocks for his buildings. This was a kind of slave labor such as prisoners of war are forced to do even now, and the Hebrews found taskmasters almost as cruel as those who bullied their distant descendants in Nazi Germany.

Their grievances came to a head when the king refused to let the tribe make a few days' pilgrimage into the desert to the east of Egypt to worship their God at the holy mountain of Horeb. Here Moses, prophet and lawgiver of the tribe, had seen the splendid vision of the

Burning Bush, of God in the form of his *shekinah*, or celestial radiance, blazing from a bush which the fire did not consume. Here, too, he had learned the marvelous Name of God, Yahweh, which none but the High Priest of the Hebrews might utter, and then but once a year in the Holy of Holies, the inmost sanctuary of the temple — the Name whose traditional interpretation is I Am.

The Book of Exodus in the Bible tells us that the Egyptian king was unmoving in his refusal to permit the pilgrimage. He remained unimpressed by the miracles which Moses and his brother, Aaron, performed in his presence — the transformation of a staff into a serpent, and the sudden appearance and disappearance of leprosy on Moses's hand. At this the God of the Hebrews visited the Egyptians with ten plagues, during nine of which the king vacillated in his decision, alternating between giving permission when the plague was at its height and refusing it when the plague had left. For Yahweh plagued the Egyptians with turning the Nile into blood, with a pest of frogs, of lice, of flies, with a murrain upon the cattle, with an epidemic of boils, with hail, with locusts, and with a darkness hiding the sun. The king was at last persuaded to let the tribe make its pilgrimage only with the tenth plague, the mysterious death of the firstborn son of every Egyptian family.

On the day before this terrible visitation of death, Moses instructed every Hebrew family to slay a lamb and to sprinkle the doorposts of their houses with its blood.

Thereafter they were to dress as for a journey, and, at nightfall, to eat the meat of the slain lamb, garnished with bitter herbs. They were to eat standing, and in haste, and be ready to depart for the desert at dawn. During that night the Destroying Angel of God visited every house in Egypt save those whose doorposts bore the smears of blood. These the Angel of Death "passed over," for the Hebrew families therein were to be "saved by the blood of the lamb."

When morning came and all the families of Egypt, including the royal family, found their firstborn sons dead upon their beds, the king was ready enough to permit the pilgrimage. By the time, however, that the tribal caravan had reached the shores of the Red Sea, a rumor reached the king that this was no mere pilgrimage. He learned that the tribe was planning to leave Egypt forever and to seek a home and an independent life of its own in the fertile country beyond the desert, in the Promised Land watered by the river Jordan.

Thereupon the king set out with chariots and cavalry to overtake the fugitives. Probably the Hebrews were expecting to detour the Red Sea, passing round it to the north. This, however, was impossible now that behind them they saw a swiftly nearing cloud of dust and heard the rumble of a thousand horses at the gallop. At this, Moses lifted up his miraculous staff over the Red Sea, and immediately its waters divided so that a path of dry land lay between them. Down this path the caravan hastened to the opposite shore. The king, at the head of his horsemen, followed by the same route, drawing closer and closer to the tail of the Hebrew caravan as it struggled up the farther slope of the seabed to the fringe of the Arabian Desert. Just as soon as the last Hebrew had left the mysterious passage through the water, Moses again lifted up his staff, at which the walls of the divided sea roared together to drown the Egyptians in the deep.

At this, Moses and all the Hebrews broke into a song of triumph:

I will sing unto the Lord, for he hath triumphed
   gloriously:
The horse and the rider hath he thrown into the sea.

The Lord is my strength and song, and he is become
   my salvation:
He is my God, and I will prepare him an habitation;
   my father's God, and I will exalt him.

Taking up the same theme, the Vesper Hymn of Easter proclaims:

The Lamb's high banquet we await
   In snow-white robes of royal state:
And now, the Red Sea's channel past,
   To Christ our Prince we sing at last.

That Paschal Eve God's arm was bared,
  The devastating Angel spared:
By strength of hand our hosts went free
  From Pharaoh's ruthless tyranny.

O thou, from whom hell's monarch flies,
  O great, O very Sacrifice,
Thy captive people are set free,
  And endless life restored in thee.

Such is the story of the deliverance of the Hebrews from captivity in Egypt, and of the origin of the Feast of the Passover, the Pesach or Pasch, which the Jewish religion observes to this day. Since the destruction of the Temple of Jerusalem by the Roman army in 70 CE, the form of the Passover has been somewhat changed. But for centuries it was kept in strict accordance with Moses's instructions to the Hebrews in the Book of Exodus, save that the lambs were slain in the Temple, and the altar rather than the doorposts sprinkled with their blood. The carcasses were then taken home and roasted, and must be eaten entirely. No bone of the lamb must be broken, and the family stood to eat, dressed for traveling.

Another important feature of the Passover was that the bread for the sacred meal must be without leavening — an observance explained by the fact that a tribe on a forced march would have no time to ferment the dough for its bread. On the assumption that the Last Supper of

Christ with his disciples was held on the day before the Passover, the First Day of Unleavened Bread (when the use of leavened dough ceased for seven days), the Roman Catholic Church still uses unleavened bread for the Mass.

Obviously the Passover is in some way connected with the ancient and widespread spring sacrifice of the first fruits of crops and kine. The lambs slain must be of the firstborn, and in the story of the visitation of the Angel of Death the Egyptian sons killed are likewise the firstborn. Behind this lies the idea that all first fruits — the first lambs born, the first crops to ripen, the first child of the family — are the special property of the gods and must in some way be offered or dedicated to them. We have noted already that the Passover, falling in the month of Nisan, is a festival of the vernal equinox.

In describing the *taurobolium*, or bull sacrifice, in the Mystery of Cybele and Attis, we saw that a special importance was attached to the spilled blood of the victim: those on whom it was poured were held to become one with Attis. The same belief accompanied the communion rite in the Mystery of Mithra, wherein bread and bull's blood were the two sacred elements. So, too, in this *criobolium*, or lamb sacrifice, it is the blood smeared on the doorposts which protects the family from death.

A simple and interesting chain of associations lies behind this belief in the magical power of blood. Among cattle-raising people, the bull or the sheep is the main source of life, and thus the form through which the divine power sustains the people. The god of the tribe is therefore symbolized *as* the animal, for the gift of life is a gift of the god's *own* life. Obviously, then, the blood, as the essential life fluid of the animal, is something mysteriously close to the divine life itself.

For this reason the Hebrews, who kept a clear distinction between divine and human life, put a taboo on blood. Blood was God's own peculiar property, and man must not drink it. Hebrew law demands that all meat be killed in the so-called "kosher" way: that is, the blood must be drained from it and poured upon the ground as a libation to God. It would appear, then, that when Jesus commanded his disciples to "drink his Blood" (that is, his divine life) in the Lord's Supper, he was pointing to a new and hitherto unknown depth of union and intimacy between man and God. The Christian may assume the divine privilege of drinking blood because he is a "partaker of the divine nature," a *son* of God, not merely a subject or servant. For to say that man is a son or child of God is to say much more than that he is created by God. It is to say that he belongs to the divine family, that divinity is in him as the blood of the father flows in the veins of his sons.

The story of the Exodus, and the Passover Feast which commemorates it, follows the now familiar pattern of the death-and-resurrection theme, although the hero of the story is a people rather than a god. The captivity of the Hebrews in Egypt corresponds to the descent of the sun into night, of the god into the underworld, or of the Creative Spirit into the Womb of Matter, where it builds the finite universe as the Hebrews built the Egyptian monuments. But by the sacrifice of the lamb and by the pouring out of its divine blood or life upon the dwellings of the captive people they are restored to freedom, the sun rises into day, and the Spirit is released from darkness.

The writers of the New Testament make much of the parallel between the Exodus story and the Christ story, identifying him both with the people of Israel and with the Passover Lamb. Shortly after his birth, Christ also goes down into Egypt, fleeing from the jealous king Herod. Indeed, St. Matthew's Gospel, in which the story of the Flight into Egypt is found, takes the parallel between the life of Christ and the history of Israel as its basic pattern. The Old Testament story is used as a "type" or prophetic symbol of the Christ story, and the Gospel is divided into five "books" corresponding to the Five Books of Moses — the Pentateuch. These are the first five books of the Bible — Genesis, Exodus, Leviticus, Numbers, and Deuteronomy — and as these contain the "Old Law" of Moses, so St. Matthew's Gospel contains the five books of the "New Law" of Christ.*

---

*   The "five books" of St. Matthew are arranged as follows: (1) Chapter 3:1 to 7:29; (2) 8:1 to 11: 1; (3) 11:2 to 19:2; (4) 19:3 to 26:2; (5) 26:3 to the end. The closing sentence of each "book" begins with the phrase, "And it came to pass that when Jesus had made an end of [e.g.,] these sayings."

St. John's Gospel stresses the parallel between Jesus and the Paschal Lamb. At the first appearance of Christ in the Gospel, John the Baptist greets him with the words, "Behold the Lamb of God, which taketh away the sin of the world." More striking still, St. John's narrative of Christ's Passion has him crucified at the very hour on the eve of the Passover when the Paschal Lamb was being slain in the Temple.

But most of the biblical references to Christ as the Lamb of God are found in the Book of Revelation. Here the triumphant Lamb is pictured as reigning in glory from the throne of heaven, adored by the hosts of redeemed souls who have been "washed white" in his blood, singing:

> Worthy is the Lamb that was slain to receive power, and riches, and wisdom, and strength, and honor, and glory, and blessing!

Here, too, is the interesting reference to "the Lamb slain from the foundation of the world," connecting the sacrifice of the Cross with a mysterious "eternal sacrifice" which occurs before the beginning of time. For we have seen that there is a parallel between the theme of Easter and the theme of the world's creation. There is the "sacrifice" of the Creative Spirit "descending" into Matter and forming the universe, which then "rises" out of the darkness of chaos. This is the "eternal" sacrifice which takes place "before" time begins. There is then the sacrifice occurring *in* time, restoring the eternal life of the Spirit which seems to have been lost in the beginning. We shall see that this correspondence between creation and salvation is our most important key to the meaning of the resurrection story.

The lambs sacrificed at the Passover had to be of the year's firstborn. St. Paul takes up this symbol in referring to Christ as "the firstborn of all creation." For Christian doctrine represents Christ as the embodiment or incarnation of the Son whom God the Father begat before time and the world were created. Beyond the earthly spring in which the first fruits of crops and kine are born, there is a heavenly and eternal spring in which the Son of God is born, and which is the life source of the whole universe. This "eternal spring" is connected with the many myths of a paradise-garden where the Fountain of Perpetual Youth flows forth from the Tree of Life. (It was in search of the fabulous land of Bimini where this fountain was supposed to be that Juan Ponce de León discovered Florida!) Christian artists have loved to represent this paradise-garden with the Cross and the crucified Christ in place of the Tree, standing above the baptismal font in whose waters the old and infirm are being transformed into youths and maidens.

The scene is described in the Book of Revelation:

And he shewed me a pure river of water of life, clear as crystal, proceeding out of the throne of

God and of the Lamb. In the midst of the street of it, and on either side of the river, [stretched] the tree of life...and the leaves of the tree were for the healing of the nations.

Revelation, describing the "last things" which come to pass after the resurrection, takes this symbol from Genesis, describing the "first things" which come to pass at the beginning of the world:

And the Lord God planted a garden eastward in Eden....And out of the ground made the Lord God to grow every tree that is pleasant to the sight, and good for food; the tree of life also in the midst of the garden, and the tree of knowledge of good and evil. And a river went out of Eden to water the garden.

For as the springtime of each year takes us back to the springtime of the world, so Easter and the resurrection take us back to the eternal spring from which all life proceeds.

THE RESURRECTION OF CHRIST

Michael Wolgemut / Hans Pleydenwurff, 15th century
Munich, Pinakothek

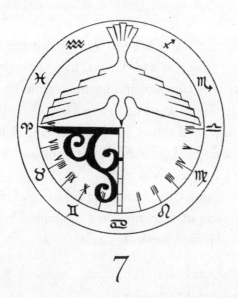

7

THE EASTER CALENDAR

If you look in the front pages of a copy of the Roman Missal or the Book of Common Prayer, you will find a Calendar of the Christian Year. You will see, however, that many of the most important Christian feast days are not included in this Calendar. The reason is that they are "movable feasts," and their dates depend on the date of Easter, which, as we have seen, changes every year. The permanent Calendar gives us only the fixed dates — Christmas and the saints' days.

The idea of the Christian Year is that the Church, in token of its union with Christ, lives through his life once every year, commemorating and reenacting its chief events. This is not just a convenient way of studying the life of Christ; it is rather a way of showing that Christ himself is living in Christians. As St. Paul said, "I live; yet not I, but Christ liveth in me."

The Christian Year, then, comprises two "cycles" — the fixed cycle of Christmas and the movable cycle of Easter. This is the Christmas Cycle:

The Advent Season (beginning the fourth Sunday before Christmas)
Christmas Day: December 25
The Circumcision of Christ: January 1
The Epiphany: January 6

The Church Year begins with Advent, not with January 1, and the Advent Season is a time of preparation for Christmas.

The Easter Cycle is more complicated. Here it is, numbered by weeks on the left-hand side:

(1) Septuagesima Sunday ⎫
(2) Sexagesima Sunday   ⎬   *The "Pre-Lenten" Season*
(3) Quinquagesima Sunday ⎭

Ash Wednesday
(4 to 8) The Five Sundays in Lent
(9) Palm Sunday
Holy Week

Lent

(10) Easter Sunday
(11 to 15) The Five Sundays
after Easter

The Easter Season

Ascension Day (Thursday)
(16) Sunday after the Ascension
(17) Pentecost, or Whitsunday
(18) Trinity Sunday
(19 to Advent) Sundays after Pentecost (or, Trinity)

The familiar doggerel of a children's hymn gives a brief and easily remembered summary of the meaning of these days and seasons of the Christian Year:

> *Advent tells us Christ is near;*
> > *Christmas tells us Christ is here.*
> *In Epiphany we trace*
> > *All the glory of his grace.*

> *Then three Sundays will prepare*
> > *For the time of fast and prayer,*
> *That, with hearts made penitent,*
> > *We may keep a faithful Lent.*

Holy Week and Easter then
Tell who died and rose again:
O that happy Easter Day!
"Christ is risen indeed," we say.

Yes, and Christ ascended, too.
To prepare a place for you;
So we give him special praise
After those great forty days.

Then he sent the Holy Ghost
On the day of Pentecost,
With us ever to abide:
Well may we keep Whitsuntide.

For our own immediate purpose one short period of a week and a day is of special importance — Holy Week and Easter. In the annual Church Calendar (sometimes called an *Ordo*), specially made out each year, the days of this period are set out thus:

Sun.	Palm Sunday
Mon.	Monday in Holy Week
Tue.	Tuesday in Holy Week
Wed.	Wednesday in Holy Week
Thur.	Maundy Thursday (of the Lord's Supper)
Fri.	Good Friday (Friday of the Preparation)
Sat.	The Holy Sabbath (Easter Eve)
Sun.	Easter Day

The arrangement of the days of the latter part of Holy Week in particular follow the account of Christ's death and resurrection given in St. John's Gospel, where, it will be remembered, Christ is said to have been crucified at the hour when the Paschal Lamb was sacrificed. But to understand the relation between the Calendar, the Christ story, and the Jewish Passover, we must not forget that the Jews reckon a day from sunset to sunset, not from midnight to midnight. Furthermore, the Jewish Sabbath is not the Christian Sunday. For Jews, the Sabbath Day of Rest is the seventh day of the week; for Christians, the weekly day of worship is the day of the resurrection, that is, the first of the week. The following table, then, will be of help in understanding how the story of Christ's Passion fits in with the Christian Calendar and with the Passover, as it was held in the year when Christ was crucified:

THE EASTER CALENDAR

CHRISTIAN CALENDAR		JEWISH CALENDAR	CHRIST STORY
Weds. in Holy Week			
	Sunset	First Day of Unleavened Bread	
Thurs. (Maundy)		13th Nisan	
	Sunset	14th Nisan The Parasceve	Last Supper
Fri. of Preparation			
	3 p.m.	Paschal Lamb slain	Death of Christ Burial of Christ
	Sunset	The Sabbath Passover meal eaten	
Sat. (Easter Eve)			
	Sunset	First Day of the Week	
Sun. (Easter Day)			
	Dawn		Resurrection
	Sunset		

To avoid confusion, it *must* be remembered that the Christian Calendar follows St. John's story of the events. For this reason the Last Supper is not, as the other Gospels would suggest, the Passover meal. St. John insists that the Crucifixion took place on the Parasceve, the Day of Preparation, when the lamb was slain but not ceremonially eaten until after sunset. Thus in the year when these events occurred, the Passover would not have been eaten until after Christ had been laid in the tomb.

With this outline of the story of the first Holy Week and Easter in mind, we can turn to the actual drama upon which this climax of the Christian Year is founded. It may seem absurd to repeat a story which is told incomparably well in the New Testament — a book which is always easily available. But though the Bible is in almost every home, it is increasingly unread. If, therefore, we repeat some of the tale of this greatest moment in history, it is not to improve upon the Gospels but to refresh the memory, and to embroider their record with some significant legends that have come down to us not in scripture but in tradition.*

---

* The reader may want to take this part of the story direct from the New Testament. If so, they will find it in Matthew 26 to the end; Mark 11 to the end; Luke 19:28 to the end; and John 12 and 13, and 18 to the end.

above

ST. THOMAS TOUCHING THE WOUNDS OF THE RISEN CHRIST

below

THE WOMEN AND THE ANGELS AT THE EMPTY TOMB

Salzburg Pericopes, Salzburg, eleventh century
Staatsbibliothek Munich

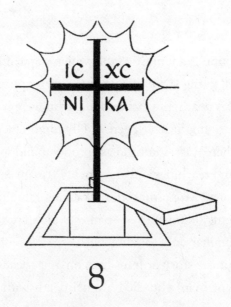

8

"HE IS RISEN!"

For nearly two thousand years the Christian world has held a strange conviction about the central character of our story. It is a story not of some remote mythological figure from a legendary past but of a man who lived in historical times. The conviction is that this man, Jesus of Nazareth, is God — the Universal Mind, the Creator and Mover of the stars — manifested in space and time in human flesh and blood. Argue as one may that this conviction is a fantastic fable which popular devotion attached to the story of a Palestinian prophet some years after his death, the fact remains that, were it not for this, the story might have been wholly forgotten. For in those days there was a multitude of prophets and seers of whose lives and teachings only fragments remain — Apollonius of Tyana, Monoimus the Arabian, Iamblichus, Mani, Epictetus, Numenius — names which are for the most part familiar only to scholars.

But the story of Jesus lives on, not because he was an innocent man who died a cruel death with bravery, for others have done as much; not because he was a great teacher of spiritual principles, for there was nothing peculiarly original in his doctrine; not even because he returned from death, for that, too, has been recorded of others. The Christ story lives because it has fascinated man's mind with the thought of a God who has shared the life of his creatures, of a King who has become his own subject. It is the revelation that the Lord of the universe is not a cruel puppet master who watches his playthings writhe in the toils of tragedies which he has plotted. It is that he himself has entered the play, has become the victim of the tragedy, and has turned it into a triumph.

The eight days of Holy Week and Easter mark out a drama, at once a History and a Mystery, which embodies both the noblest and the deepest vision of God to which human thought can reach.

PALM SUNDAY. This is the day on which Jesus and his disciples came to Jerusalem, the Holy City of Judea, after he had finished his teaching in the smaller cities and villages of Palestine. As this was the first day of the week in which the Passover was held, people were coming into Jerusalem from hundreds of miles around, crowding its steep and narrow streets, and pitching their tents at the foot of the walled and fortified hill on which the city stood.

By this time Jesus had acquired considerable fame in Palestine as a prophet and healer, and there were many who felt that he might be the long-expected Messiah who would free the Jews from Roman imperialism and restore the temporal and spiritual power of the People of God. The rumor of his arrival in Jerusalem at this important season gave rise to a wave of excitement and speculation. As Jesus approached the city, riding upon an ass,* an enthusiastic crowd met him with branches of palm and olive which they had cut from trees along the highway, waving them and shouting, "Blessed is he that cometh in the Name of the Lord! Hosanna in the highest!"

MONDAY, TUESDAY, AND WEDNESDAY IN HOLY WEEK. During these days the arrival of Jesus in Jerusalem began to have momentous results. The religious rulers of the city were alarmed about him. On the one hand, they were afraid that a popular Messiah without military power

---

* To ride upon an ass rather than a horse signified that one came not as a military conqueror but in peace.

(which Jesus obviously despised) would achieve nothing but quick and severe reprisals from the Roman government. On the other hand, they suspected Jesus of the serious sin of blasphemy, for it was rumored that he claimed to be divine, the very incarnation of God's Wisdom and Word. This impression was strengthened by the tone of authority with which he taught and acted in the Temple, where, in the sight of the crowds gathered for the Feast, he had expelled the money changers and overturned their tables.

Therefore the chief priests of the Temple and the rulers of the city decided that Jesus must be "put out of the way." To this end they made a secret arrangement with Judas, one of Jesus's disciples, to betray his Master. Perhaps Judas was impatient with Jesus for producing none of the signs of worldly power that were expected of the Messiah, and hoped by bringing him into direct conflict with the authorities to force his hand. For thirty pieces of silver Judas agreed to show them where they might find Jesus alone, without a friendly and possibly dangerous crowd around him, so that he could be arrested without disturbance.

MAUNDY THURSDAY. Jesus instructed his disciples to find a room in the city where they could eat the Passover meal, and here, on the evening after the First Day of Unleavened Bread, they all ate supper together. At the beginning of the supper, Jesus announced his discovery that one of his disciples would betray him. Without letting the others know who the betrayer was, Jesus turned a little later to Judas and said simply, "What thou doest, do quickly." At this Judas left the room, the others thinking that he had been sent to buy something for the feast, since he was the keeper of their common funds.

Toward the close of the meal, Jesus, certain now that he was about to die, took a loaf in his hands and asked God's blessing upon it. Breaking it in pieces, he distributed it among them saying, "This is my Body which is given for you." After this he handed them the large common wine cup. "Drink ye all of this," he said. "For this is my Blood of the New Covenant* which is shed for you and for many for the forgiveness of sins. Do this as oft as ye shall drink it, in remembrance of me."

When supper was over, they left the house and went outside the city to a garden by the Mount of Olives called Gethsemane. Here Jesus spent the remainder of the night in prayer until shortly before dawn, Judas, who must have known Jesus's intention of going to Gethsemane, came with the officers of the Jewish rulers. Judas identified Jesus with a kiss, whereupon the officers seized him and took him to the Jewish court of the Sanhedrin. His disciples fled for their lives.

---

* That is, the new relationship between God and man signified by the drinking of blood, a relationship not of lord and servant but of father and son.

GOOD FRIDAY. Examining him in regard to his divine claims, the Sanhedrin convicted Jesus of blasphemy, and took him to Pontius Pilate, the Roman governor, to have him sentenced to death on the ground that he claimed to be "King of the Jews." In the meantime, the Sanhedrin sent out "rabble-rousers" to defame Jesus's character among the crowds in the streets and to stir up popular indignation against him. They managed to get together a sufficiently impressive and angry mob to make Pilate nervous. Then — as now — a crowd hungry for sensation could easily be moved to thoughtless anger or enthusiasm by a clever mob orator, and, fearful of a serious disturbance, Pilate granted the request that Jesus be sentenced to death, although he could not understand that there was any real charge against him. Throughout the proceedings, Jesus made not the least attempt to defend himself.

Pilate then handed Jesus over to the Roman guard. Having first flogged him, the soldiers made a crown of thorny twigs and put it on his head. They clothed him in a purple robe and made mock obeisance to him. Thereafter they stripped off the robe and marched him outside the city, making him drag the heavy wooden cross on which he was to be nailed, until they came to a hill called Golgotha — the Place of the Skull. And here, under the blazing heat of the midday sun, they nailed him to the cross by his hands and feet, tied him firmly to the crossbeam with ropes, and set him up to die horribly and slowly from exposure and loss of blood.

Legend tells that the wood of this cross had a strange history. It is said that after Adam and Eve had been expelled from the Garden of Eden, one of the sons of Adam, named Seth, had managed to obtain a cutting from the fatal Tree of Knowledge whose fruit had opened his parents' hearts to evil. Some versions of the legend say, however, that the branch was from the Tree of Life, which also stood in the Garden. From this branch a staff was made, a staff handed down from generation to generation among the ancient Hebrew patriarchs. This was the staff which Moses turned into a serpent before the Egyptian king, the staff with which he opened the passage in the Red Sea, and struck the rock in the wilderness so that it gave forth water. And when the Hebrews, escaped from Egypt, were plagued by snakes in the desert, this was the staff on which Moses hung a serpent of bronze that all who gazed upon it should be healed of the plague. This, too, was the staff of the shepherd Jesse, the father of David, which miraculously blossomed as a sign that his son should be king. After many adventures, the staff came at last into the hands of Joseph, husband of Mary. By his son, James, it was given to Judas Iscariot, and by him to those who used it to fashion the Cross of Christ. "The tree," wrote St. Augustine, "which had brought about the fall and the loss of Paradise, shall be the instrument of redemption."

Such is the legend of the Holy Rood, or Rod, of the Tree which bears both the fruit of death and the fruit of life and around which has been formed one of the most fascinating collections of Christian symbolism. Associated with the Tree are two serpents, the serpent of poison and the serpent of healing. The one is Lucifer, the Devil, who tempted Eve to eat the fruit of Knowledge. The other is Moses's serpent of bronze which healed the plague, and which Christ used as a symbol of himself. To this day, bishops of the Eastern Orthodox Church carry a pastoral staff shaped not, as in the Western Church, like a shepherd's crook, but like the Caduceus, the rod entwined with two serpents — emblem, also, of the art of healing.

One must read the unforgettable story of Christ's agony on the Cross from the Gospels themselves — of the Seven Last Words, of the soldiers gambling for his garments, and of the two thieves that were crucified on either side of him. Toward three o'clock in the afternoon the light of the sun began to fade. Darkness covered the land, and the earth quaked and split. In the Temple of Jerusalem, at the very moment of the Paschal sacrifice when Jesus gave up the ghost, the great veil covering the entrance to the Holy of Holies tore asunder from top to bottom. Through the rent thus made, the *shekinah*, the radiance of God, fled from the sanctuary of the Chosen People that had now rejected him.

For reasons which the story does not make too clear, Jesus died rather sooner than most victims of crucifixion. He may have lapsed into a coma and been actually killed by the spear which one of the soldiers thrust into his side so that water and blood poured from the wound. Ordinarily the victim's legs were broken, but St. John says that he was killed like the Passover Lamb whose bones must remain intact.

Before sundown, the beginning of the Sabbath, he was taken down from the cross. Joseph of Arimathaea, a man of some wealth who had known Jesus and sympathized with him, begged his body from Pilate and carried it to a tomb in his own garden. One of the most notable legends of Western Christianity says that Joseph of Arimathaea had acquired the cup with which Jesus had celebrated the Last Supper. In this cup, known as the Holy Grail, he gathered the blood that still dripped from the five wounds in Christ's body. After the resurrection, the Grail is said to have come to Europe, and medieval lore abounds with stories of the heroic knights who went in quest of this sacred relic.

THE HOLY SABBATH. We have learned that the Jewish Day of Rest is our Saturday, when, for the devout Jew, all work is forbidden. During this day Jesus rested in the tomb, and St. Matthew tells us that the Sanhedrin set guards by its sealed stone door to be sure that the disciples would not steal away the body. There had already been rumors that he would rise from the dead, and, should they be given any credence, further disturbances might arise among the people.

One passage in the New Testament (Peter 3:19) states that after his death Christ "went and preached unto the spirits in prison." Upon this is founded the story that on this Holy Sabbath Christ descended into Sheol, or Hades, the realm of the past, the underworld where dwelt all those who had died since the days of Adam. Here he is said to have performed the great "harrowing of Hell," entering its barred gates and releasing Adam, Noah, Abraham, Isaac, Jacob, Moses, all the patriarchs and prophets, and all the souls of the just, from the dominion of death.

EASTER DAY. Early on the morning of this, the first day of the Jewish week, our Sunday, some of the women who had been associated with Jesus came to the tomb with ointments and spices to anoint the body.

They found the guards fast asleep, the tomb open, and the body vanished. On the floor lay only the linen bandages in which it had been wrapped.

As they looked up from the floor of the tomb they beheld two angels in garments radiant with light. In instant terror the women lay prostrate on the ground, but the angels said, "Why seek ye the living among the dead? He is not here, but is risen!" Shortly afterward, Mary Magdalene was walking alone in the garden, bewildered and weeping, when she saw someone whom, in the dim morning light, she took to be the gardener. "Woman," he said, "why weepest thou?" And she replied. "Sir, if thou hast borne him hence, tell me where thou hast laid him, and I will take him away." At this the man spoke one word — "Mary!"

Recognizing the voice of Jesus, Mary cried out, "Master!" and rushed to embrace him. But he checked her, saying, "Do not cling to me, for I am not yet ascended to my Father. But go to my brethren, and say unto them that I ascend to my Father and your Father; and to my God and your God."

It would take too long to tell the many stories of the appearances of the risen Christ to his disciples. On two occasions he came to them while they were still in hiding, mysteriously entering a room with closed doors, and yet eating with them in a most unghostlike fashion. For forty days he came and went among them — a Christ tangible like flesh and blood, yet volatile as a spirit. They saw him for the last time on the Mount of Olives, where he vanished from their sight into the mist.

"DO NOT CLING TO ME!"

The Risen Christ appears to St. Mary Magdalene
Martin Schongauer, fifteenth century
Colmar

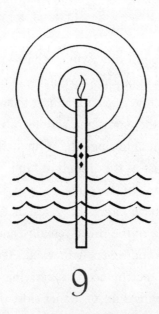

9

A THOUSAND YEARS
AFTER

For the last time before Easter the high altar of the Cathedral glows with white and gold. It is a thousand years since the first Maundy Thursday, at the dawn of the Middle Ages, when, in some great shrines, clergy and monks and people were still keeping the rites of Holy Week and Easter with full splendor and fervor. In the place of Christ is the bishop, standing at the center of the altar, and in the place of the Apostles his canons and clergy stand around him, while others kneel below him in the choir and upon the steps that lead up into the lofty apse of the sanctuary. In soft, almost inaudible, tones the bishop repeats the words and actions of Christ with the Bread and Wine. He sings the "Our Father," and, after a hymn to Christ as the "Lamb of God," distributes the holy Bread among his brethren.

When all have eaten, he gives thanks and blesses them. One piece of the Bread remains, and this he places in a golden cup and covers with a veil. As he lifts it from the altar he is met by acolytes carrying lighted tapers, and, accompanying him on either side, they and all the monks and clergy in the choir form into a procession and leave the high altar for a distant part of the great church. As they move slowly between the towering pillars their chanted hymn fills the high vaults of the roof with running echoes, until they come to a side chapel, to a small altar brilliant with flowers and lights. Here the bishop sets down the golden cup, for this is the Garden of Gethsemane and the holy Bread is Christ. Here, then, monks from the cloister adjoining the Cathedral will take turns to watch in prayer for the rest of the day, and all through the night until Good Friday morning.

As the day draws toward evening, the monks gather in the Cathedral choir for vespers, and when these are done the bishop and his attendants go again to the high altar. The choir sings:

They parted my garments among them,
And upon my vesture they cast lots

and the bishop strips the altar of its white and golden cloths as Christ was stripped for crucifixion. He puts out the candles and takes down the candlesticks, leaving the sanctuary drab, dark, and bare.

When the bishop returns from the altar the choir sings again:

Mandatum novum do vobis — A new commandment I give unto you: that ye love one another as I have loved you.

It is from this first word, *mandatum* (commandment), that Maundy Thursday gets its name, for the Maundy is the ceremony of foot-washing which the bishop now begins. Like Christ washing the feet of his disciples before the Last Supper, he takes off his outer vestments, girds himself with a linen towel, and takes an ewer of water in his hands. Before each one of his brethren he kneels, pours a little of the water on his right foot, wipes it with the towel, and kisses it.

After dark, a triangular stand bearing fifteen candles is set before the stripped altar, and the monks gather in the choir for the singing of Tenebrae, which means "darkness." Despite its stark simplicity, the world knows few more exquisite acts of worship. The choir begins the psalm, "Why do the heathen so furiously rage together?" They sing it to the restrained, contemplative, quietly flowing melody of the Gregorian chant, in which there is a sort of thrilling sadness. It runs on, verse after verse repeating the same cadence, and the repetition brings a strange peace, like the sound of waves washing the shores of an ocean. As each psalm ends, one of the fifteen candles is extinguished. Christ is being deserted by his disciples. One by one they leave him in the darkness of Gethsemane.

For a space the sequence of the psalms is interrupted, and they sing from the Lamentations of Jeremiah:

> *They say to their mothers, Where is corn and wine?*
> *when they swooned as the wounded in the streets*
> *of the city....*

> *Jerusalem, Jerusalem, return unto the Lord thy God.*

> *O my vineyard, my chosen, did I not plant thee?*
> *How then art thou turned into such bitterness?...*

> *Jerusalem, Jerusalem, return unto the Lord thy God.*

> *O all ye people, behold and see if there be any sorrow*
> *like unto my sorrow. Is it nothing to you, all ye*
> *that pass by?*

Echoes, it seems, from the Babylonian hymn of mourning for Tammuz, thousands of years before:

A tamarisk that in the garden has drunk no water,
  Whose crown in the field has brought forth no blossom.
A willow that rejoiced not by the water-course,
  A willow whose roots were torn up.
A herb that in the garden has drunk no water.

Again the psalms continue. The candles go out, and next they put out the tapers in the choir stalls. The whole church is now dark save for one candle left burning on the stand before the altar — Christ alone with every disciple gone, denied even by Peter. They chant the song of Zacharias, "Blessed be the Lord God of Israel," and at the end, the one remaining candle is taken away and hidden behind the high altar. Christ, Light of the World, is hidden in the tomb.

In total darkness the monks kneel and intone, very softly, the Fifty-first Psalm, "Have mercy upon me O God, after thy great goodness," and as it ends a single voice continues with a brief prayer. There is a sudden, sharp noise, as of a heavy tile falling to the floor, and the one remaining candle is returned to its place on the stand — a promise of the rending of the tomb and of the return of Christ from death. In silence all rise and leave the Cathedral.

On the morning of Good Friday they assemble again before the high altar, where there hangs a great wooden crucifix draped in black. Attired in black vestments, the bishop and his deacon and subdeacon approach the altar and kneel. Prayers are said, and then they begin to sing the story of the Passion of Christ from St. John's Gospel. The singing is a form of drama, for the bishop sings the part of Christ, the deacon sings the narrative parts, the subdeacon the parts of Pilate and other members of the drama, while the whole choir sings the words of the Hebrew multitude.

After further prayers have been sung, the bishop unveils the great wooden crucifix, crying, "Behold the wood of the cross, on which was hung the Savior of the world!" And the choir answers, "O come, let us adore!"

"Behold the wood!" Does the essential story of the Mysteries ever change? Here at last is the noblest form of the pine of Attis and the tamarisk of Osiris. The bishop lays the crucifix before the altar, takes off his sandals, kneels and kisses it, and in this all the clergy and monks follow him, one by one, as well as lay folk from the city and the surrounding countryside. As they reverence the wood of the Cross, the choir sings again from the Lamentations, holding still to the tradition of the Mysteries:

O my people what have I done unto thee, or wherein have I wearied thee? Testify against me.

And there follows the hymn to that Tree of Life in which the ancient myths find their fulfillment:

Faithful Cross, above all other,
One and only noble Tree;
None in foliage, none in blossom,
None in fruit thy peer may be.

When all have venerated the Cross, a procession forms with the bishop and goes to the side chapel, where, throughout the night, the sacred Bread of Christ's Body has been watched amid lights and flowers. Reverently the bishop takes the golden cup again in his hands and, surrounded with tapers and incense, carries it back to the high altar, while the choir sings the hymn, *Vexilla Regis*, written by Venantius Fortunatus nearly five hundred years before:

O Tree of beauty, Tree of light,
O Tree with royal purple dight,
Elect on whose triumphal breast
Those holy limbs should find their rest.

At the high altar the bishop prays, takes the censer and swings incense about the golden cup. In silence he consumes the holy Bread, and with dramatic suddenness the service ends. The congregation leaves, and the Cathedral remains bare and deserted save for the wooden crucifix above the altar.

Late on the night of Holy Saturday the Cathedral is as dark as death, and yet people are beginning to tiptoe silently into the nave.* In the intense darkness they cannot see the decorations, the flowers, the mass of candles on the altar, that have been set out in readiness for Easter Day. Toward midnight they hear the clink of steel striking on flint at the back of the church. From the rock comes fire; from the tomb, Christ. Sparks from the flint catch on tinder and are blown into flame. The bishop murmurs the prayer for the blessing of the New Fire. From the flame the deacon lights one branch of a triple candle which he carries upon a reed, and as it lights he sings on a quiet, deep note, "The Light of Christ!" And the choir answers, "Thanks be to God!"

The single light is carried to the middle of the church. There is a pause while the second branch of the candle is lit. Louder now, and upon a higher note, the deacon sings again, "The Light of Christ!" and there comes the answer, "Thanks be to God!" They move up to the entrance to the sanctuary, and here the third branch is lit. This time the deacon almost shouts it, "The Light of Christ!" and the choir responds with its full force, "Thanks be to God!"

---

* In the modern Roman Catholic rite the ceremonies of Holy Saturday and the First Mass of Easter take place at 10 a.m. on Saturday. But all the words of the service suggest darkness as its setting. The ancient practice, still continued in the Eastern Orthodox Church, was to celebrate the Easter Mysteries at midnight. The Orthodox service employs the same symbolism of light in darkness. Every member of the congregation carries a candle, and the service includes a great procession round the outside of the church. The rites described here are perhaps not exactly those of 1000 CE, but a more or less idealized version of the practice of the Western Catholic Church over many centuries.

Now there is standing, at the left side of the altar, an enormous candle, almost six feet high, in a proportionately large candlestick. This is the Paschal Candle, which is to represent the light of Christ upon earth after his resurrection. The deacon goes to the foot of this candlestick, and here begins the most exultant and splendid chant in all the music of the Church:

> Rejoice now all ye heavenly legions of angels: and celebrate the Divine Mysteries with exultation: and for the King that cometh with victory, let the trumpet proclaim salvation. Sing with joy, O earth, illumined with this celestial radiancy: and enlightened by the King eternal, thy glory, believe and know that thou hast put away the darkness of all mankind!

As the chant goes on, the deacon sets five grains of blessed incense in the stem of the candle, in representation of the five wounds of the crucified Christ. Before he lights the candle, he sings of the mystery of the light which comes out of darkness:

> Now is come the night whereof David said: Behold, the night is as clear as the day: then shall my night be turned into day...

— words that take us back to the Mysteries of Demeter at Eleusis, where the night upon which the initiation was completed was called "that holy night, clearer than the light of the sun." So, too, the initiate of the Mysteries of Osiris said, "About midnight I saw the sun brightly shine."

To implement his words, the deacon lights the Paschal Candle, and immediately attendant acolytes put tapers to the flame and, going to the altar, the choir, and all parts of the Cathedral, carry the New Fire of Christ to every candle. The church is now filled with light — light which the people will take home for their own fires. The deacon brings his chant of triumph to a close:

> We pray thee, therefore, O Lord most merciful: that this Candle...may continue to shine forth without ceasing, and may vanquish all the shades of darkness. That being accepted before thee as a sweet savor, it may be numbered with the lights which thou hast kindled. May the Day Star find it burning when he dawneth into day: the Day Star that riseth and knoweth not his going down: but coming forth from the place of darkness gladly giveth forth light unto all creation.

While the bishop reads the prophecies of Christ's resurrection from the Old Testament, the candidates for the Christian initiation of baptism make themselves ready about the font at the west end of the church. The Paschal Candle is taken down from its candlestick and carried in solemn procession to the place of baptism, as the choir sings the psalm. "Like as the hart desireth the water-brook, so longeth my soul after thee, O God."

Calling upon the almighty and eternal God to "be present at these Mysteries," the bishop begins the chant for the blessing of the font, whose waters are identified with the primordial Waters of Chaos from which all life emerged in the beginning of time:

> Therefore I bless thee, O creature of water, by the living God, by the true God, by the holy God, by that God who in the beginning separated thee by his Word from the dry land, whose Spirit moved over thee.

He divides the water with his hands and throws some of it to the four points of the compass, calling to mind the four rivers that flowed out from the Tree of Life in the Garden of Eden.

And then, in token of the entry of the Spirit into the waters, he breathes upon their surface and, taking the Paschal Candle, he plunges it thrice into the font, saying:

> May the power of the Holy Spirit descend into all the fulness of this font.

The act is rich in symbolic meaning: it is Christ descending into, and being born from, the womb of the Virgin Mary, "the immaculate womb of this divine font"; it is Christ going down into death, and rising from it again the third day; it is the descent of the Spiritual Sun into the Material Waters for the creation of the universe.

Thus consecrated, the holy water is sprinkled upon

the people with a bunch of rushes, and then is mixed with sacred oils. Thereupon the catechumens, young and old, who are to be baptized come forward. They kneel before the bishop, who signs them on the brow with the Cross for the casting out of all evil, and proceeds to question them as to their faith in God, and his Son, and his life-giving Spirit. He signs them also upon all the organs of sense and the limbs of the body, "that ye may have life everlasting and live forever and ever."

To complete the initiation they come one by one to the font, where the bishop takes up the water in a shell and pours it thrice over their heads, saying to each, "Peter," "John," "Mary," "Anastasia — I baptize thee in the Name of the Father and of the Son and of the Holy Spirit." This done, he anoints them with oil, clothes them in white robes, and to each gives a taper lighted from the Paschal Candle. Thereafter he takes them to the steps of the sanctuary before the high altar, and here, sitting in his episcopal throne, he lays his hands upon their heads as they kneel before him one by one, conferring upon them the interior fire of the Holy Spirit.

It is now drawing toward dawn. The high windows of the Cathedral are faintly luminous with the returning blue of the sky. Having taken upon themselves the gift of union with Christ, the newly baptized are now to witness for the first time the inmost mystery of Christianity, the celebration of the Eucharist (thanksgiving) that we are one with his substance (the Body) and his life (the Blood).

While a litany is sung, the bishop ascends to the altar, and his deacons change their vestments from purple to white and gold. They bring incense to him, and as the smoke from the censer hangs above the altar candles like a light-filled cloud, the choir sings:

> *I am risen, and am present with thee, alleluia!*
> *Thou hast laid thine hand upon me, alleluia!*
> *Such knowledge is too wonderful and excellent for me,*
> *alleluia, alleluia!*

Soon the bishop raises his voice, and with a strong chant begins, "Glory be to God on high! —" And as the choir takes up the hymn, "— and on earth peace to men of goodwill," all the bells in the Cathedral tower crash out together and run again and again down the scale, like happy children released from school running down the steps to play in the street. For they have been silent since Maundy Thursday.

As the risen sun now bathes the arched roof of the church in light, Easter Day reaches its climax in the stately ritual of High Mass — the hallowing of the Bread and Wine, the communion of the clergy and people, while the choir sings:

> *Christ our Passover is sacrificed for us, alleluia. Therefore*
> *let us keep the feast with the unleavened bread of*
> *sincerity and truth, alleluia, alleluia!*

The Christian Mystery is complete. The bishop turns from the altar and dismisses the congregation, "Depart in peace, alleluia, alleluia!" And with the answer, "Thanks be to God!," the people receive his blessing and hasten out into the clear light of day.

10

EASTER IN FOLKLORE

A multitude of popular customs, many of which survive among us today, are derived from the Christian Easter story, from the rites of the Church, and from pagan observances which existed in Europe long before Christian times. In modern America the one Easter custom that appears to be really universal is the donning of new clothes. But the crowds who join in Easter parades, dolled up in their new finery, are doubtless unaware that they represent a last dim survival of the conferring of white robes upon the newly baptized. We may be sure that in the far-off days when this was the general practice, those already baptized put on new or clean garments at Easter as a reminder of their own baptism. Together with the fact that the Feast was, in any case, an occasion for general rejoicing and "putting on the dog," it is easy to see how the observance became what it is today.

If we go once again through the Calendar from Maundy Thursday to Easter Day, looking not at the Church but at popular custom, we shall see many practices which have come into being in more or less the same way. Since, however, their number is legion, we can only select some of the more interesting and significant.

MAUNDY THURSDAY. Coming directly from the rite of the Church is the so-called "Maundy Custom," observed in slightly differing form in many parts of Europe. As the bishop, or, in smaller churches, the priest, ceremonially washed the feet of his clergy and congregation, it became the custom for persons of rank to perform a similar office for the poor. It is recorded of many of the kings of England that, on Maundy Thursday, they washed the feet of as many poor men as they were years old, and at the same time distributed gifts. In 1361 King Edward III, then fifty years old, gave fifty pairs of slippers to fifty poor men. Queen Elizabeth I conducted a similar ceremony amid considerable splendor, washing the feet of a number of poor women in a silver bowl of holy water scented with flowers, and thereafter gave them presents of money, food, and clothing. In later times the ceremony degenerated into a simple gift of money, and today the King's Lord High Almoner — the Archbishop of Canterbury — gives silver coins, specially minted for the occasion, to as many poor folk as the king is years of age.

Maundy Thursday is likewise the day when the church bells become silent until Easter, and it is a general European folk belief that at this time the bells take flight for Rome. Their absence is considered an occasion for some caution against the powers of darkness, since it is thought that the sound of the church bells acts as a repellent to evil spirits and to ill weather. But it is said that the bells go to Rome to "make their Easter," to "visit the Pope and dine with him," to "make their confessions," or to "look for the eggs which they will drop on their return." When, on Easter Day, they ring out again, one must bend down and embrace one's chair or bench, if in church, or, if out in the fields, one must fall down and embrace the earth.

Other names for Maundy Thursday are Shere, Sheer, or Chare Thursday — forms of an early English word for "clean." The practices of washing feet and stripping the church altars and washing them have suggested the suitability of this day as a time for housecleaning. Thus, if one were to observe the times and seasons in the most exact way, Maundy Thursday would be the appropriate day for beginning one's spring cleaning.

GOOD FRIDAY. God's Friday, Long or Great Friday, is far more rich in folk customs than the day preceding. As might be expected, the symbolism of the Tree plays a prominent part in these customs. In Northwestern Europe these customs are particularly associated with the mountain ash tree, and it is barely possible that this goes back to the Norse mythology of Yggdrasil, the fabulous ash tree at the center of the world, whose branches reached heaven, and whose roots lay in the underworld, gnawed by the worm Nidhug. It is said that Odin, or Wotan, the Norse supreme God-All-Father, learned the secrets of divination by spearing himself to this tree in a sort of crucifixion.

> *I know that I hung*
> *On a wind-rocked tree*
> *Nine whole nights,*
> *With a spear wounded,*
> *And to Odin offered*
> *Myself to myself;*
> *On that tree*
> *Of which no one knows*
> *From what root it springs.*

Thus there are widespread practices of gathering the branches of the mountain ash on Good Friday and putting them on the doorposts as a protection against evil. For the tree is credited especially with powers against witches, against the ague and snakebite, for it is, of course, by the Sacred Tree that the serpent of Evil is conquered.

In the Southern states of America there is a Good Friday legend about the dogwood tree, usually in flower at this time of year. It is said that the dogwood was once a great tree like the oak, and that its wood was so strong that it was used for the making of Christ's Cross. But the tree was heartbroken at being used for this purpose, so that Jesus, as he hung upon it, said to the tree, "Because of your regret and pity for my suffering, never again shall the dogwood tree grow large enough to be used as a cross. Henceforth it shall be slender and bent and twisted, and its blossoms shall be in the form of a cross — two long and two short petals. And in the center of the outer edge of each petal there will be nail prints, brown with rust and stained with red, and in the center of the flower will be a crown of thorns, and all who see it will remember."

Presumably because of an association between Christ and fire, it is considered most unlucky in the Isle of Man to poke the fire with an iron poker on Good Friday. A stick made of the mountain ash is used instead, and all the fire irons are hidden away. In some places blacksmiths refuse to drive nails on this day. Among other "unlucky" things to do on Good Friday, it is believed among some fisherfolk that ill fortune will betide anyone who goes fishing on this day. This might easily be explained by the ancient and well-known connection between Christ and the fish. The origin of this symbol is that the Greek word for fish, *ichthys*, is made up of the initial letters of the words "Jesus Christ: God's Son: Savior" (*Iesous CHristos THeou Yios Soter*).

It is natural, too, that the day on which Christ was buried should be regarded in many places as a good time for sowing seed. Some people believe that any seed put in the ground on this day will thrive, but in England the belief is especially attached to parsley, for "if you want to have parsley all the year round it must be sown on Good Friday." Another "lucky" thing to do on this day is to break crockery. It is sometimes said that every jagged edge will pierce the body of Judas, and in Corfu there is a custom of throwing crockery down a steep hill on Good Friday, at the same time uttering curses against Judas.

Unlike Maundy Thursday, Good Friday is often considered a bad day for washing. Clothes hung on the line will be brought in spotted with blood, or the suds will turn to blood, or a member of the family will die.

In England the most notable Good Friday custom is the baking of hot cross buns, which are almost universally eaten for breakfast on Good Friday morning. These are buns, or spiced rolls, round in shape, with a cross indented in the top. The custom is said to have originated in 1361 at St. Alban's Abbey, when one of the monks baked them as gifts for the poor. At one time these buns were sold by street vendors who went through the towns early on Good Friday morning, crying:

Hot cross-buns, hot cross-buns,
One a penny, two a penny, hot cross-buns;
Smoking hot, piping hot,
Just come out of the baker's shop;
One a penny poker, two a penny tongs.
Three a penny fire-shovel, hot cross-buns!

All kinds of beliefs prevail as to the curative properties of the Good Friday buns. Unlike common bread, they are supposed not to grow moldy when kept, and stale buns are retained for all kinds of purposes — for grating into medicines, as charms against shipwreck, as a means of keeping rats out of the corn, and as a general "good luck" talisman for the household, to be hung from the ceiling on a string.

It is not at all unlikely that there is a popular association between the hot cross bun, or Good Friday Bread, and the Mass Bread. Such an association would very simply account for the supernatural powers attributed to it and would be natural in view of the fact that the Mass Bread is almost always impressed with a cross.

HOLY SATURDAY. The folk customs of Holy Saturday, or Easter Eve, are more especially connected with the rites of the Church. It has been pointed out that the more ancient practice of holding these rites at night has largely been dropped and that nowadays the Blessings of the New Fire and the font are held on the morning of

Easter Eve. It is natural, then, that most of the popular observances of this day are connected with fire and water, since it is an almost universal custom in Roman Catholic countries for the people to take the blessed fire and water for use in their homes.

Fire from the Paschal Candle is in general used for rekindling the household hearth on this day. A common belief is that any piece of wood, or any taper, originally lighted at this source will, when relighted, serve as a protection against storms.

Not only is the holy water blessed at the font on this day carried home in bottles, but in many places the priest goes outside the church to bless the cisterns, ponds, lakes, and rivers of the neighborhood. Widespread is the belief that, at the moment when the font is blessed or when the bells ring out at the Mass of Easter Eve, *all* water becomes holy, though the belief is connected principally with running water. At this moment the women gather at fountains and springs to wash in the water that flows out, as a protection against disease, or to take it home in vessels for sick persons to drink.

Separate from the ecclesiastical custom of blessing the New Fire is the practice of lighting the so-called Judas Fire in the churchyard. It is usually kindled from a brand consisting of blessed palms from Palm Sunday, and its principal fuel is generally wooden crosses from the cemetery which have fallen down during the past year. Sometimes an effigy of Judas is burned in the fire.

The bonfires of Easter Eve are particularly common in Germany, where they are lighted not only in church-yards but upon hilltops, where the young people gather around them, dance, sing Easter hymns, jump over them, and sometimes light straw wheels from their flames and set them rolling down the hill. Boys will run through the fields with flaming straw bundles from the fire, in the belief that such fields will become especially fruitful in the following year.

In Bavaria this popular ceremony is called "burning the Easter Man." The fire is kindled on high ground near the village, and is built around a tall cross wrapped in straw to look as though a man were upon it with his arms outstretched. It is set alight from a taper bearing New Fire from the church, and on Easter Monday the cold ashes are gathered and scattered on the fields.

Arising, no doubt, from the custom of bringing eggs for the priest when making one's Holy Saturday confession, is the children's game of Pace-Egging — a means of collecting the eggs. (The name of this game is, of course, a corruption of "Pasch-Egging.") Groups of children, usually boys, will go around the neighborhood dressed in outlandish costumes to dance and act simple plays in return for which they expect to receive eggs and other gifts. The words of these playlets are traditional rhymes, like the following, sung when one of the conventional characters of Pace-Egging mummery steps in for her part:

> *The next that steps in is Old Miser Brown Bags,*
> *For fear for her money she goes in old rags.*
> *She has gold, she has silver, all laid up in store,*
> *She's come a-pasche-egging and hopes to get more.*

In France the Pace-Egging rhymes have, as a rule, somewhat more reference to Easter. They are sometimes performed by the choir boys of the local church, and their making the rounds of the village is not unlike the Christmas custom of carol singing.

> *Good women, who to God would fare,*
> *Bring us each of eggs a pair,*
> *A good ham, too, for a gift this day*
> *Makes sure, good women, that your hens will lay;*
> *And you'll go straight to your heavenly rest*
> *As the hen herself goes straight for the nest.*

On a similar theme, another French rhyme runs:

> *Eggs for the little children, pray!*
> *Four for me and eight for my pal —*
> *And you'll go straight to Eternal Day*
> *As a stone to the bottom of a well.*

A large number of these rhymes employ, somewhat incongruously perhaps, the traditional Easter exclamation of joy — "Alleluia!"

I've a little cock in my basket;
It'll sing for you if you ask it
With eggs red and white, Alleluia!

EASTER DAY AND EASTER HOLIDAYS. In the "high and far-off times" before so many Christians learned to confuse goodness with gloom, the festivities of Easter Sunday, even in their lightest mood, began in the church itself. Odd as it may seem to us, there was an Easter game played "in choir" by clergy and even by bishops. Its origins are very mysterious, but it appears to have been some kind of ball game where the reverend fathers stood in a circle and played "catch." Some of the accounts of this game indicate that it was played with eggs, and records of such an affair are found in connection with Chester Cathedral in England. "The bishop and dean took eggs into the cathedral and, at certain stages in the service, engaged in an egg-throwing match with the choristers. Later, they all retired to dine on gammon of bacon and tansy pudding."

In the course of time such pranks withdrew from the sanctuary and became the popular egg-throwing and -rolling games conducted on village greens. Their explanation is possibly the simple one that hard-boiled eggs may thus be conveniently and amusingly cracked for eating. No clear record seems to exist of the egg ever having had a ritual use in church, although one old parish in the City of London preserves the custom of giving each member of the Easter Sunday congregation an egg bearing the words, "My Redeemer."

The fact that almost all churches now have parish halls attached to them is, in part, the result of excluding another Easter festivity from the church itself. This was the Easter "Church Ale," a convivial distribution and drinking of ale after the principal Easter service, the money derived from it being used for repairs to the church fabric. It is perhaps fanciful to connect the origin of this custom with the primitive Christian *Agape*, or Love Feast, which disappeared from common use long before Christianity came to Western Europe. But it is certain that Church Ales easily degenerated into brawls and for this reason were ordered out of the church itself. As a result, church houses were built or rented adjoining the church, and equipped with kitchens and drinking utensils. Some of these ultimately became taverns, while many more were retained for what is now the normal social life of the church community.

A festive act which, where it remains at all, still goes on in the church itself is the Easter Miracle Play — a dramatic reenactment of the story of the resurrection (distinct from the rites described in the last chapter). Nowadays this is usually performed in the afternoon by the children of the church school. Formerly it was an adult enterprise, as is indicated by an entry in the books of an English parish in the year 1561: "for brede and ale for them that made the stage and other things belonging to the play, 1s. 2d."

We shall not be surprised to find many folk beliefs associated with the Easter sunrise, in view of the Feast's ancient connection with the dawn of spring. All over Western Europe it is held that the sun dances at dawn on Easter Day, and in many places groups of people climb to the top of a nearby hill to watch the dance. They are not always disappointed, for if you stare at the sun for a short time it will seem to revolve and change color. Another common belief is that, at the same time, the image of the Lamb of God with the red cross banner appears in the sun, while in France it is sometimes said that the rays of sunlight penetrating the dawn clouds are angels dancing for joy at the resurrection.

Likewise, all over the United States and in many parts of Europe, the Easter sunrise is the occasion of popular services, held on some convenient hill or elevated ground in the crisp air of a spring morning. We say "popular" services, for this is no part of the traditional Christian Liturgy but rather a custom which many of the Protestant Churches have adopted in response to a general demand. Some ancient instinct seems to move even in the sophisticated soul of modern man, driving him out from his comfortable bed into the dim light of early morning to praise God at the dawn of spring. It has thus become the one special Easter observance of Protestant Christendom which — aside from the floral decoration of the Church — distinguishes the worship of Easter from other Sundays of the year.

A custom which seems to bear a direct reference to

Christ's resurrection after three days in the tomb is the so-called "Easter Lifting." This consists in lifting a person thrice into the air, and must be done between 9 a.m. and noon on Easter Monday and Easter Tuesday. On Easter Monday the women are lifted by the men, and, on the day following, the men by the women, and the usual payment for this service is giving a kiss to every member of the group that lifts you. In the Low Countries, however, the observance is sometimes a spanking instead of a lifting. Elsewhere an Easter "prank" played between men and women is shoe stealing, the stolen shoes being redeemed for a small forfeit the following day or evening. Usually the women retaliate by stealing the men's caps rather than their shoes or firmly laced boots.

Just because it is a time of festivity, Easter is also the occasion for many other games, hunts, dances, and feasts, which, having no special connection with Easter, might be observed at any other time of rejoicing.

Folk custom both imitates and stimulates the regular and official rites of a religion. By imitation it carries the message of those rites from the church to the field and fireside and weaves the ritual drama of the Savior-God into the fabric of everyday life. It symbolizes the truth that religion is not something which belongs only in church, but something to be taken out of church and translated into the terms of farming and cooking, of eating and playing.

On the other hand, when a religion such as Christianity comes to a people from outside, it adopts and "baptizes" some of the folk customs which derive from older religions. It selects and weaves into the Liturgy folk observances which seem to signify the same eternal principles taught by the Church. And this symbolizes the truth that religion is not something which comes to a man from outside alone, but something which he can only receive if there is already a light in his heart to respond to its message. "To him that hath shall be given."

EARLY-MORNING EASTER MASS

Alan Watts

11

THE SECRET OF
THE SYMBOLS

As a diamond has many facets, so the meaning of Easter may be understood from many points of view. Looking into the heart of a diamond to behold its interior fire, we watch the intense spark of light change from red to blue to white as this or that facet is turned uppermost. As the fire in the diamond is many-colored, so the meaning of a great spiritual symbol has many dimensions — some of which cannot be put into words at all. Others cannot be expressed save at considerable length, having a complexity such as the interpretation of Easter which is given by Christian theology. To do justice to this interpretation, and to describe it in terms intelligible to the average modern man, is a feat impossible within the span of a few pages.

Obviously the rites of Easter have some connection with mankind's perennial joy in the renewal of the earth's life at springtime. But this is a very dim and partial glimpse of the truth behind the symbols. We can turn the diamond so as to get a more vivid light, even though its color must be but one of many.

Looking back over our story, two points stand out clearly. One is that the new life which the risen Savior brings to man is not just ordinary, biological life alone. This is true whether the Savior be Christ or Osiris. The gift of Easter is not mortal life, but eternal life, spiritual life. The second point is that the bestowal of this gift is the fruit of death. *Stirb und werde* — die and come to life — this is the essence of the story. It is like learning to float on the water. So long as you tense your muscles and try to hold your body upon the surface, you sink. But as soon as you try to sink, you relax and float. It sounds crazy, but it works. In the familiar language of the Gospel: "Whosoever would save his soul shall lose it, but he that loses [we might say, *looses*] his soul shall find it."

From the standpoint of everyday common sense, there is something about eternal and spiritual realities which gives one the feeling of having stepped, like Alice through the looking-glass, into a world where everything is back to front and topsy-turvy. "Die and come to life." "The first shall be last, and the last first." "He that humbleth himself shall be exalted." "Except a grain of corn fall into the ground and die, it remains alone; but if it die, it brings forth much fruit." This is what Easter is saying: the source of life — not ordinary life alone, but eternal life — is death itself. The source of supreme joy is something which, at first sight, seems to be utter despair.

There was a time when almost every holy man adorned his reading desk with a human skull which seemed to say, "Remember, O man, that dust thou art and unto dust thou shalt return." Nowadays we regard this as a sort of perverse wallowing in gloom, for so-called "healthy mindedness" urges that we thrust aside every thought of the inevitability of death. Common sense moves us to hold fast to life so long as its brief passage permits. But that life flows from our clutching fingers like swift water, and in the anxiety to check its elusive flight we hang on to it like grim death. Wrestling to cling to ourselves, and to all that is ours, we strangle ourselves with fear.

Is it any wonder that the skull seems to laugh? "Why torment yourselves?" it says. "You *cannot* hold on; you cannot save yourselves. Why, you would not want security even if you could have it, for all living things are changing things, and all that is changing is dying. Give yourselves up, for what else can you do?" At which all robust common sense revolts and cries, "Give up? Never! Why, this is the most spineless and abject surrender to despair!" And so common sense does not notice that the skull is laughing not *at* the holy man but *with* him.

For he has discovered the strange secret of the topsy-turvy land of wisdom — that the greatest treasure is always found in the very place where it is least expected. The King of Kings is born in a cowshed. For the means of life and salvation he employs death upon a thieves' gibbet.

Thus from giving oneself up, common sense expects nothing but despair. To admit — without hastily thrusting the thought away — that clinging to one's life is a futility and an illusion, that in reality it simply cannot be done, this would seem to be the end of faith and hope alike. On the contrary: to admit this is, for the first time, to live. If the symbols of Easter do not convey this at least, they convey nothing.

It is a truth which anyone can prove by experiment that just as soon as the terrible anxiety to hold on to yourself is given up as useless and impossible, it is like getting instant relief from an agonizing cramp. It is like the opening of a dam — a dam built in the heart to shut in and hold the flow of life, where the water lies stagnant and still. Once the dam is opened, the water of life runs shouting, sparkling, and crystal clear through the soul. For that joyous stream does not have to be sought out in distant places; it does not have to be *made* to flow by persuading oneself into a happy or hopeful frame of mind. It is simply *here*, within and all around us, a pressing and ever-present Spirit, waiting for the dam to open.

"And he showed me a pure river of water of life, clear as crystal, proceeding out of the throne of God..." Only poetry and symbol can even attempt to describe that strange, unexpected transformation that invades a man's whole being, as if from out of the blue, when he knows that he can do nothing but let go of himself. Its many names — eternal life, the Spirit of God, the indwelling Christ, the victory over death — may perhaps give some dim hint of this indescribable deliverance from one's own world of self-centered mortality into the "kingdom which is an everlasting kingdom." Happily, to describe and try to imagine it is unnecessary. When the dam is open, it is simply *there* — a thing already given — and words are as redundant as red paint on a rose.

This is but one of many reasons why Christians keep Easter not just as a hope or as a reminder of a great precept and example, but as the celebration of a triumph. For the passage from Good Friday to Easter Day is the passage from the full acceptance of death to the dawn of real life. This is no mere expectancy, but a vision enjoyed here and now, a vision which accounts alike for the self-denying charity of the saint and the fearless joy of the martyr.

If, then, there is one symbol in which the whole meaning and mystery of Easter may be summed up, it is water. From the spring rains to the baptismal font, from the waters of chaos in which the world began to the water of eternal life flowing from the throne of God, this symbol lies uppermost in the pagan and Christian Easters alike. It takes precedence over the egg, the lily, the lamb, the peacock-phoenix, and even the hallowed fire.

Resisting it, one sinks; giving in to it, one floats. Struggling vainly against the river of life, it seems a torrent of doom sweeping all to certain death. Yet to him that is willingly carried on its flood it becomes, of a sudden, the eternal life of God, sharing with him its vast resources of power. Humble, like Christ, it seeks the lowest level, but there is nothing which it cannot overcome. Like the Lamb of God led to the slaughter, it resists neither nails nor blows, yet they have no power to harm it.

According to the myth, the world is made in water. From water comes all life, and by water life is maintained. In the fountain of baptism the world is redeemed, and whosoever drinks of the water from the throne of God lives forever. Small wonder, then, that for so many centuries Christians have begun the celebration of Easter singing:

I SAW WATER FLOWING FROM THE RIGHT SIDE OF THE TEMPLE, ALLELUIA: AND ALL TO WHOM THAT WATER CAME WERE MADE WHOLE, AND SHALL SAY: ALLELUIA, ALLELUIA! O GIVE THANKS

UNTO THE LORD FOR HE IS GRACIOUS: BECAUSE HIS MERCY ENDURETH FOR EVER. GLORY BE TO THE FATHER, AND TO THE SON, AND TO THE HOLY GHOST: AS IT WAS IN THE BEGINNING, IS NOW, AND EVER SHALL BE UNTO ALL THE AGES OF AGES. AMEN.

AFTERWORD

The production of *Easter* occurred during the year of 1949, culminating in its publication in 1950 by Henry Schuman, Inc., in New York. Alan (my father) and Eleanor (my mother) were going through a divorce during that time. Alan was under a great deal of stress over having to leave the Church and his post as chaplain of Northwestern University and uncertainty about his financial future. The book almost didn't get published because Alan and Henry Schuman were at odds about the concept — would it be "religious" or "folkloric"? Henry wanted the latter. Alan agreed, under duress, to include a bit of the folkloric.

During this time, I was summarily sent off to boarding school. My father sent me off with a lovely small leather prayerbook and Bible (King James version), with the inscription "Joan Watts, with love from her father, September 14, 1949." The following March, I received a copy of *Easter* with the inscription (seen at the beginning of this book) "...I do not want you ever to be afraid of death, whether it be the death of people or the death of old times which we have loved," referring, I believe, to the breakup of our family.

In reviewing *Easter* for possible republication this year, I noticed an artwork in the book attributed as "Modern Indian (artist unknown)" (see page 30 in this edition). Alan was also a talented artist and calligrapher, and I believe this painting is definitely by my father, even though he attributed it to an unknown artist. I realized I had in my possession two other similar watercolors by my father, both representing Easter. One is finished, the other is not, and I think he had intended to include them in the book, but for reasons unknown, did not. The similarity in style of these works to the "artist unknown" piece is undeniable.

I am grateful to our editors, Jason Gardner and Kristen Cashman, who thought we should include them in this edition. The first, completed artwork (on page 120) depicts an early-morning Mass, presumably Easter. Notice the dark earth in the foreground with a sprinkling of pebbles and flowers. If you look above that, on the right side you can see a pair of bunnies, and on the left a squirrel. Alan's folkloric concession to Henry Schuman? The other painting (on page 42) is of the Crucifixion. The dark earth foreground is not completed. It, too, would have had pebbles and flowers. I have yet to come across the original of the "Modern Indian (artist unknown)" work. Why Alan preferred to list his work as "artist unknown" I have no idea.

Joan Watts
Bellevue, Idaho
November 14, 2022

INDEX

ABOUT THE AUTHOR

Alan Watts is best known as an interpreter of Zen Buddhism in particular and of Indian and Chinese philosophy in general. He earned the reputation of being one of the most original and unfettered philosophers of the twentieth century. He was the author of more than twenty books, including *The Way of Zen*, *The Wisdom of Insecurity*, *Does It Matter?*, *Psychotherapy East and West*, *The Book*, *This Is It*, *The Joyous Cosmology*, *In My Own Way*, and *Tao: The Watercourse Way* (with Chungliang Al Huang). He died in 1973.